Exploring Careers in the Computer Field

By
Joseph Weintraub

The Rosen Publishing Group, Inc.
New York

Published in 1983, 1985, 1988, 1990, 1993
by The Rosen Publishing Group, Inc.
29 East 21st Street, New York, NY 10010

Revised Edition 1993

Library of Congress Cataloging in Publication Data

Weintraub, Joseph, 1943–
    Exploring careers in the computer field.

    Includes index
    (Exploring careers)
    1. Electronic data processing—Vocational guidance.
    2. Computers—Vocational guidance. I. Title. II. Series:
Exploring careers (Rosen Publishing Group)
QA76.25.W46   1983   001.64′023   82-21491
    ISBN 0-8239-1601-4   ISBN 0-8239-1717-7 (paperback)

Manufactured in the United States of America

This edition has been updated to reflect the ever-changing and expanding computer field. The variety of computers, programs, and jobs available is much wider than when the book was first published. The new information incorporated into this revision includes a chapter on future career trends, an updated list of colleges offering computer science majors, an expanded glossary reflecting current terminology, and a list of computer associations and societies.

About the Author

Joseph Weintraub is the founder and president of Thinking Software, Inc., a small consulting firm in the field of artificial intelligence. He is a graduate of the City College of the City University of New York and is a member of Mensa. He has been engaged in data processing since 1968.

Mr. Weintraub has been a programmer for *Time* magazine, a systems manager for Abraham and Straus, a senior analyst with the Metropolitan Transit Authority, a data processing instructor at New York University, and an adjunct lecturer in Computer Science at Pace University. He has also written articles for *AI Expert*, *AI Magazine*, and *PC/AI Magazine*.

In recent years, Mr. Weintraub has developed artificial intelligence programs that "fooled" the judges into thinking they were conversing with human beings. Two of his programs, PC Therapist III and PC Professor, won the Loebner Prize in both 1991 and 1992 at the annual artificial intelligence competition held at the Boston Computer Museum.

Mr. Weintraub lives with his wife and two children in New York City.

Contents

1

The New Computer World

Businesses today rely on computer technology to assist them in almost every area of corporate life. Computers have invaded grocery stores, fast-food restaurants, big businesses, and small offices. They process data, store information, work out complex mathematical problems, track inventory, and even control temperature and lighting in office buildings. Reliance on the high-speed digital computer is so complete that the world of commerce would grind to a sudden halt if computers were removed.

Early computers were extremely large and very expensive. They were difficult to program and broke down frequently. The first large digital computer was developed during World War II for the U.S. Army. Called the Electronic Numerical Integrator and Calculator (ENIAC), the machine was enormous—100 feet long, 10 feet high, and 3 feet wide—and, according to one of its developers, would "fail at least once a day."

Smaller computers were developed during the 1950s, and there was a push for corporate use. The Prudential Insurance Company of America began using a computer to maintain life insurance policy files. The Chrysler Corporation tracked spare auto parts with a computer, and General Electric Company used one for inventory control. Although still used primarily by the government, computers had moved into the world of big business.

By the 1960s, almost every large company had made a substantial investment in a computer center of its own, usually built around a large-scale IBM 360 mainframe. The Apple computer invaded homes and classrooms during the 1970s, and in 1981 International Business Machines introduced the IBM Personal Computer, or PC, which became enormously successful. This was followed by a newer, faster generation of computers called the IBM Personal System 2 (PS2).

Today, personal computers dominate the computer industry, with annual worldwide sales of $93 billion. Hundreds of companies are involved in development and sales of personal computers. Some are working on their own designs; many are cloning (copying) the designs of established companies like IBM.

The source of much of this recent revolution is the business office, where huge strides have been made in harnessing the power of computers. Word processing is a standard and accepted replacement for the typewriter, and other forms of office automation are becoming increasingly popular. It is probable that someday you will work in an office, and it is equally probable that someday you will use a personal computer.

"Personal computers have created the first true standard for office automation," asserts a leading company president. "American business has already invested billions of dollars in this method of office automation, and an entire industry is bringing new technologies and advances into the market for these workstations."

The established applications for the personal computer include word processing, spreadsheets, desktop publishing, electronic mail, and a full range of accounting functions including general ledger and accounts payable and receivable. More recently, artificial intelligence applications, usually in the form of expert systems, have become available.

ARTIFICIAL INTELLIGENCE

Development of artificial intelligence, or AI, became popular during the 1980s. Artificial intelligence is a branch of computer science that deals with enabling computers to replicate human thinking. AI attempts to emulate certain aspects of human behavior, such as reasoning and communicating. It also tries to mimic biological senses, including sight and hearing. Although interest in AI dwindled in the late 1980s, it is again increasing. According to an industry analyst, "Despite the recession, we've heard more enthusiasm from companies currently using expert systems than we have in the last five years."

With growing interest in AI will come a need for programmers, systems analysts, and managers who are knowledgeable in the workings of AI. Already a $600 million industry, AI is expected to grow by 20 to 30 percent by the end of the century. Important new career paths created by its growth will be sales, training, knowledge engineering, programming in AI languages such as LISP (List Processing) and PROLOG (Programming Logic), and systems analysis to integrate these new tools into an advanced management information system.

The three types of AI software that are generating the greatest enthusiasm among users are expert systems, psychological analysis, and pattern recognition.

Expert Systems

Expert systems are programs that can imitate the reasoning process of a human expert in a specific field, such as medicine or finance. Because the systems attempt to automate processes of judgment and decision-making, they are often called knowledge-based systems or rule-based systems. Expert-system construction begins with interviews with experts to determine the reasoning they

3

use in solving problems. Expert-system shells or toolkits are available at reasonable prices. These are "empty" expert systems, ready to be loaded with a knowledge base by an acknowledged expert in a specific field. Expert systems are especially useful to managers in the areas of finance and manufacturing, where the ability to "crystal-ball" future trends can be valuable.

Psychological Analysis

These programs attempt to measure human traits, such as extroversion, kindness, nervousness, and intelligence. An example is Jury Selection Expert, a psychological analysis program that can provide prosecutors with a personality profile of the ideal juror for a case, as well as some questions that might reveal objectionable candidates. Other psychological analysis programs are used in personnel offices to evaluate staff members and in credit offices to assist managers in making fast and accurate decisions in commercial credit situations.

Pattern Recognition

This software is designed to enable computers to recognize patterns the way people do. During a process called optical character recognition (OCR), a computer can "read" printed material with an optical scanner. The scanner determines the shapes of the characters, and the computer software translates the shapes into computer text. Speech recognition, or voice recognition, refers to a computer's ability to recognize spoken words. The Kurzweil Applied Intelligence Corp., for example, has developed a speech-recognition product call VoiceMed. Doctors use it to dictate medical reports and create instant medical charts. The product is in use by about 600 hospitals around the United States.

DESKTOP PUBLISHING

Another revolution created by the power of the com-

4

puter is in publishing. Desktop publishing is the use of a personal computer for the writing, layout, and printing of documents that normally would have required a typewriter and professional printing facilities. It employs a computer and specialized computer programs to combine text and graphics to produce a document that can be printed on a laser printer or a type-setting machine. With desktop publishing, any company or person can lay out a finished newsletter or book and print large numbers of professional-looking copies at a moderate price.

Desktop publishing has been associated chiefly with the Apple Macintosh Computer, which is characterized by a "what you see is what you get" video screen. The Macintosh has a high-resolution video screen that is capable of displaying exactly what will appear on the printed page, including graphics, special type fonts, and photographs. Typically, the Mac runs special desktop publishing software such as Postscript and directs its output to a 300-dpi (dots per inch) laser printer.

OTHER PC USES

What else do people use personal computers for? Many use them simply for entertainment, to play colorful, exciting video games such as Star Wars, Space Invaders, or Dungeons and Dragons. Increasingly sophisticated chess programs are being developed for the microcomputer; a chess grand master recently was defeated by a computer in tournament-level play. Income taxes and personal financial record-keeping are made easy with software such as Lotus 1-2-3. Many users find color graphics very tempting, and software such as Painter and Multiview 24 make computer art accessible to everyone. The software program Action! even allows users to create animated presentations on a personal computer.

With the addition of a modem and a telephone line, the personal computer can dial into a world of information, shopping, and free computer programs ready to download and run. These services are available through such commercial databases as The Source or through the many free bulletin boards run by hackers (computer hobbyists). It is also possible to communicate directly with Dow Jones to receive the latest stock quotations and instantly calculate the current value of a securities portfolio.

Household automation, including meal preparation, climate control, and energy conservation, is increasingly possible. Sophisticated home security systems, including burglar alarms that automatically dial a phone call at the first sign of an intruder, are now home computer–based. Computer-aided education for children (and adults) teaches math, spelling, and hundreds of other subjects, including—of course—programming. The personal computer is the first home appliance that teaches the user how to use it.

Many people run financial applications such as payroll or general ledger for a small business carried on at home; quite often the product is new personal computer software. Some hobbyists enjoy composing music on the computer, and the power of the PC to create the sound of an entire orchestra is actually worrying some professional musicians. Word processing and desktop publishing software can assist in the preparation of reports or newsletters and is becoming available for almost every personal computer. With Phase II Sales Success profile, employers can use a computer to weed out job applicants with poor sales potential.

Advancements are also being made in the area of multimedia applications. Someday soon in your living room, your personal computer, high-definition television, stereo, VCR, and laser disks will be joined into a new multimedia information and entertainment system. Already, compact disks run on computers hold encyclopedias, cookbooks, and other information. Computers are available that respond to spoken commands, instead of commands typed at a keyboard, making computer use possible for those unable to use their hands or eyes.

Computer firms continue to discover more ways that computer technology can assist both businesses and individuals with day-to-day activities. These firms are not only investing in the development of personal computers, but also focusing on the development of mainframes and minicomputers.

Whether you are planning a career in a business, technical, or creative field, your future will be influenced by computer technology. During the past decade, computers have become essential in fields like banking, insurance, accounting, and finance. Today, even the fields of music, art, and publishing are embracing this incredible machine. If you are in high school now, it can be virtually guaranteed that you will someday own a home computer. By the time you graduate from college, it is very likely that you will know how to program in BASIC, the most popular PC language.

Computer programming became the hot new career choice in the 1980s. Although the job market is somewhat tighter for trainees today, there are many computer-oriented jobs to be had. The challenge is to find the right one for you.

Companies evaluating college graduates for potential jobs are shifting their focus from the purely technical and are seeking students with well-rounded educations emphasizing business problem-solving. This means that future computer science graduates will be expected to have more knowledge of accounting, management, administration, and marketing. They will be expected to come up with new and innovative solutions to business problems using personal computers, minicomputers, or mainframes.

The College Placement Council reports that beginning salaries for college graduates in the computer field are between $29,123 and $35,153 a year. The wide variety of computer-related occupations includes:

Computer Operator
System Help Desk Representative
Computer Programmer
Systems Analyst
Software Engineer
Computer Salesperson
Chief Computer Programmer
Data Communications Technician
Computer System User Support Analyst
Computer Systems Hardware Analyst
Computer Security Coordinator
Data Recovery Planner

A complete list can be found in the *Dictionary of Occupational Titles*, published by the U.S. Government Printing Office. The DOT is available in government bookstores and in most college and public libraries.

2

The Computer Career Guide

Computer programming is one of the few professions still hungry for good people. In today's difficult job market, the want ads still show hundreds of openings for programmers. According to the *Occupational Outlook Handbook*, "Employment of Programmers is expected to grow much faster than the average for all occupations through the year 2005 as computer usage expands."

Starting salaries average between $17,000 and $21,000 a year, and once in the profession, advancement can be very rapid. Experienced full-time programmers earn about $34,000 annually, and many on the managerial level earn $60,000 or more. Equally important as salary is job satisfaction and involvement. Programmers describe their jobs as challenging and exciting. There is a sense of accomplishment in doing well a difficult job that money cannot replace.

Computer careers are possible for anyone. If you have a logical mind and the willingness to work hard, you can begin climbing the data processing ladder to success. If you are in a dead-end job or unemployed, if you are a student and uncertain about your future, data processing is for you. If you are an executive who fears being replaced by a computer, or a housewife planning to reenter the job market, data processing is for you.

The data processing field has turned into an enormous industry. It is now the largest single industry in the

President
Vice President
Manager of Data Processing
Systems Manager
Manager of Programming
Operations Manager
Software Engineer
Computer Programmer
Computer Operator
Data Control Clerk
Computer-peripheral-equipment Operator
Keypunch Operator

The Data Processing Ladder to Success

United States, employing one out of every ten workers. The opportunities are fantastic. The Sunday help-wanted section of any metropolitan newspaper lists more jobs under Programmer than in any other single category. There are also many ads under the headings Systems Analyst, Data Control Clerk, Operator, and Project Leader—all related fields, all dealing with the computer.

Hundreds of employment agencies make their entire income by putting the right computer professional in the right place at the right time. Many of these agencies are devoted strictly to the placement of data processing professionals. Many of the consultants who staff the agencies earn $30,000 to $40,000 a year after only one or two years' experience in the field. How do they do it? They work on commissions averaging over $1,000 per placement. One a week is all they need.

The most lucrative field of all, however, is computer sales. The people who actually sell and lease the computers manufactured by IBM, Honeywell, NCR, Burroughs, Univac, and several minicomputer makers are in such a high bracket that they rarely reveal their incomes. One young salesman who covered the Wall Street area for IBM was actually able to retire after only seven years of major sales. So whether your final career turns out to be in programming, systems design, operations, or even personnel placement or computer sales, a solid knowledge of computer careers will be a valuable asset.

Here are some examples of people who have found rewarding careers in data processing:

Richard J. has a high school diploma. "I was working on the Ford assembly line. It was back-breaking, boring work with no future. One day they speeded up the assembly line. I had a fight with my foreman and got fired. I talked over my future with my wife and got an office job as a data control clerk, working closely with programmers and systems analysts. At night I read every book I could get my hands on about programming. One year later, one of the programmers left for a better position and I moved right up. Now I earn $28,000 and feel good about my work."

Edward D. is from a poor minority-group family and never even finished high school. "I was working in a big real estate office as a clerk, taking home about $100 a week. The computer operator there taught me how to operate the IBM 360, and after a while I became night operator. I went to a programming school for a few months, and now I am earning real good money at an insurance company."

John S. went all the way to a BA in psychology before he found out that the degree was not very valuable. "When I finally got my degree I was on top of the world. Then I found out that the only thing it qualified me for was to be a caseworker for the city Welfare Department at $12,000 a year. I tried it for a while and couldn't take it. I got into a company that offered a training program in data processing, and today, after five years, I'm earning $27,000 a year and doing really interesting work."

Frank S. went from nothing to real success in the computer field. "I bummed around in college and never graduated, but luckily I took a few programming courses. When I gave up on college, I got a job as a programming trainee for $18,000. I liked the work and learned everything I could about computers. I liked getting things done right, and pretty soon I discovered I had a knack for management. Today I am married and have three kids and a house in Scarsdale. I am president of a computer firm, and I'm worth over a million."

How do you know if data processing is the right field for you? Many types of people are successful in data processing because there are so many types of opportunities. But in general, you should be alert, intelligent, logically oriented, and good in math. If you like playing chess or backgammon, you will like computer programming.

THE SEVEN RULES FOR GETTING INTO COMPUTER PROGRAMMING

If you have a college degree in mathematics or computer science, you will have no problem in getting a trainee position as a computer programmer for about $18,000 a year. If you don't have the degree, don't let it stop you. Plenty of people in the programming field have only a high school diploma, and many have risen to the management level. Here's how to do it.

1. Get a job in a company that uses computers.

Most large companies have computers, and more and more small to medium-sized companies are beginning to use them. It is easier to get a promotion to programmer at a company where you have made friends than to walk in off the street and apply for a programming job when you have no experience.

2. Get as close to the computer as possible.

If you can get a job as a data control clerk, that is ideal. You will be working closely with one or more programmers and can learn from them. Find out who hires the programmers and get to know him or her. Someday that person may be interviewing you. Best of all, once you are in the data processing department, many companies will pay part or all of your tuition for night-school studies in computer programming.

3. It is easier to become a computer operator than to become a computer programmer.

Learn to run a computer. If you are a data control clerk, there will be ample opportunities to work after business hours. Take advantage of them. Spend as much time as possible in the computer room. Get to know the second- and third-shift operators and ask questions. If they want to take a break, offer to stay and keep an eye on the computer. They will tell you what to do. Find out how they learned to operate computers and do the same thing.

4. It is easier to start on the second or third shift.

Most computers run twenty-four hours a day. The second shift runs from five until midnight; the third shift, from midnight until eight in the morning. For obvious reasons, there is more turnover among employees who work these hours. This is the easiest path into a good job in data processing. If your company is hunting for a night operator, tell them you know how to run the computer and that you want the job. Don't be shy! Night work may be inconvenient, but it won't be forever. After a few months you may be able to switch when there is an opening on the day shift, and someday you will make that move into programming.

5. Learn as many computer languages as you can.

The more languages a programmer knows, the more marketable his skills are. The main languages in order of importance are COBOL, RPG II, BASIC, Assembly, FORTRAN, and PL/1. Don't stop studying until you have learned them all. If possible, purchase a personal computer and use it to increase your programming skills.

6. The more you do, the more valuable you are.

The greater your responsibility and day-to-day involvement with the business of your company, the greater your job security and promotability become. Work can be fun, and no one ever got fired for working too hard.

7. Don't look for a job when you have one.

Job-hoppers are common in the data processing field, but with every jump they will find it harder and harder to put together a reasonable looking résumé. It is difficult, if not impossible, to tell what a job is like until you have tried it, so unless there is a big problem in the company you are with, stay at least three years. The longer you are with a company, the more responsibility you can assume. The more you learn about the business, the more valuable you become. When there is no possibility of further growth in your company, then make your move.

COMPUTER EDUCATION

You have probably seen ads on TV for commercial data processing schools urging you to enroll and take their courses in programming. I have one word of advice on the subject: don't! In the many years I have been in the field, I have never met anyone who got a programming job through a commercial trade school. Instead, get the catalog from your local college and enroll in the data processing courses one or two at a time. It is not necessary to work toward a degree or certificate in data processing, but if it is possible, it certainly looks well on your résumé.

Here are the courses to take, in the order you should take them:

1. **Introduction to Data Processing.** This course is an introduction to the fundamentals of information processing, including computer hardware and software. Additional subjects are flowcharting and applications of computers to commercial and scientific problems. Computer programming in the BASIC language is frequently included.

2. **COBOL Programming.** This course focuses on techniques for applying the COBOL language to solution of business problems. COBOL is by far the most important data processing language. Many successful data processing professionals know only COBOL. During a COBOL course, programs are flowcharted, coded, compiled, tested, and documented. Details of the sequential and index-sequential access methods are discussed, and the course usually includes an introduction to table handling and searching techniques.

After completing these two courses you will have a clear idea of your aptitude and interest in programming. If you decide to continue, the most valuable additional courses will be Advanced COBOL, RPG II, Systems Analysis, and Assembly Language. At this point you should be ready to write your résumé and find out what your newly acquired skills are worth in the job market.

One good thing can be said about the commercial data processing schools. If you are just out of high school and want a job fast, some of the commercial schools have a course that will teach you to operate a computer. Since most colleges don't teach computer operations, this is one area in which the trade schools remain useful. While in any school, get to know your teacher as well as possible. If he is a college instructor, he may also work for a company and may help you break into the field if you impress him with your hard work and intelligence. Sometimes part-time jobs are available right at the university computer center, giving you the opportunity to combine your studies with on-the-job experience.

DATA PROCESSING POSITIONS

Now let's take an in-depth look at the various positions within a typical data processing department. A data processing department can have fewer than ten employees or more than two hundred, but all departments have certain similar positions. At the top is the Vice President of Data Processing, who serves a liaison function between the DP department and Finance or Accounting. Reporting directly to him is the Director of Data Processing, who is more involved in the day-to-day operation of the department. Three managers report to the Director: the Manager of Systems and Programming, the Manager of Operations, and the Manager of Technical Support.

16

The Manager of Systems and Programming has Systems Analysts, Project Leaders, and Programmers on his staff. The Manager of Operations has Shift Supervisors, Computer Operators, Data Control Clerks, and a Tape Librarian on his staff. The Manager of Technical Support has Systems Programmers and a Data Base Administrator on his staff. Now let's look at some of these positions in detail.

Position: Data Control Clerk
Educational Requirements: High school diploma
Aptitudes: Logical mind, attention to detail
Salary Range: $12,000 to $22,000 per year

Computers do not make errors, but keypunch operators and programmers sometimes do. The function of the Data Control Clerk is to discover these errors before the incorrect reports are distributed to users all over the company. He or she is responsible for balancing and checking out all reports that come off the computer. This is accomplished through use of a book called the control log, which contains documented balancing procedures for each computer job. In addition, the Data Control Clerk is often required to track down the error to a specific input card, correct it, and resubmit the computer job.

Data Control is a necessary and important function, but because the job tends to be low-paying and somewhat boring, it is not recommended as a career choice. It is, however, an excellent stepping-stone into Operations or Programming. Some large corporations periodically offer programming aptitude tests and free training to those who get the highest scores.

Position: Computer Operator
Educational Requirements: High school diploma

Aptitudes: Ability to operate the computer, good health, mechanical skills

Salary Range: $15,000 to $30,000 per year

The Computer Operator is one of the hardest workers on the data processing team. His job is to keep the computer running at full capacity at all times. That means keeping the "Wait Light" off. The Wait Light is a tiny red light on the computer console that flickers when the computer is not being used to full capacity.

His bible is the book of Run Instructions. This is detailed documentation on how to run each system, usually prepared by the Systems Analyst and Programmers who originally created the system. Each day the Operator is responsible for running both production jobs and tests. Production is the normal daily work of the installation; it may include systems such as Payroll, General Ledger, Accounts Receivable, and Inventory. Tests are trial runs of new systems still in the programming phase.

Because computers are so expensive, they generally run twenty-four hours a day, seven days a week. That means that Computer Operators typically work on a shift basis. One scheduling approach is to have the Operator work twelve hours a day for three days and then take four days off. Some companies have the Operator work an eight-hour day and five-day week but rotate night shifts every three months. The point is that Computer Operators rarely work a standard nine-to-five day for very long.

It should be pointed out that the typical Operator's job is physically quite demanding. He is always on the go, carrying heavy boxes of paper, mounting disk packs, and carrying stacks of computer tapes to and from the tape library. Because of this, an Operator must be fairly strong and healthy. The Operator must also be mechanically inclined, for most of his day is spent working with machinery. This does not mean there are no female Computer Operators, but they are in a very definite minority.

The Computer Operator can make or break the installation. One mistake—mounting an incorrect tape, for example—can cause errors that may not be discovered for months and when finally tracked down will be virtually impossible to correct. So a fast and accurate Computer Operator will always have a secure job and always find his abilities in demand.

Position: Computer Programmer
Educational Requirements: College degree in computer science or mathematics desirable
Aptitudes: An extremely logical mind and knowledge of one or more computer languages
Salary Range: $25,000 to $60,000 per year

The Computer Programmer's primary function is to write coded programs that control the computer. These programs can be written in COBOL, BASIC, FORTRAN, RPG II, Assembly, or any one of another dozen languages. COBOL (COmmon Business Oriented Language) is the most often used. It looks very much like English but must be coded much more precisely, according to specific rules.

On a typical day the Programmer is assigned to work with a Systems Analyst, who gives him a set of specifications for a program. These specifications serve the same function as the blueprint that an architect gives an engineer. The Systems Analyst designs the program, but the Programmer actually creates it. A programmer on my staff once said, "Programming is like building a machine out of ideas!"

After receiving the specifications from the Analyst,

the Programmer reads them and then thoroughly discusses them with the Analyst, clearing up any points he might not completely understand. Specifications vary widely from company to company. At one company the specifications may be extremely detailed and run well over a hundred pages. They may map out almost all of the logic and leave only the coding for the programmer. Another company may rely almost entirely on brief verbal specifications.

In either case, after thoroughly understanding the specifications, the programmer may flowchart his solution. Flowcharting is a visual aid for mapping out complex logic. The next step is coding, usually on a special coding pad designed specifically for the language being used. In more modern installations, the Programmer may enter his code directly into a CRT (cathode-ray tube), creating his program online without the use of paper or pencil. Writing a program can take several hours or several months, depending on what the program is intended to do and how complex it is. When coding is complete, the program is submitted to the compiler. The compiler is a manufacturer-supplied software program that translates the Programmer's English-language statements into the machine language required to operate the computer. Compilation is repeated several times until perfect, and then the testing phase begins. Testing can proceed with actual live data or with a representative selection of test data that the Programmer creates himself. The goal is to test completely all the various logical paths within the program. If logical errors are discovered, the program must be debugged or corrected.

Testing usually takes place in two phases: the unit test, in which the program is tested by itself, and the systems test, in which the program is tested as part of a complete system made up of many programs. When the output of the program has been verified as complete and accurate, it is documented, put into production, and turned over to operations. The Programmer may be called on occasionally for program maintenance or modification. If sometime in the future his program bombs out or fails, he will probably be the one asked to correct it. Many Computer Programmers have written hundreds of programs for one company, and soon find themselves in secure and rewarding positions with excellent career prospects.

Position: Systems Analyst
Educational Requirements: Bachelor's degree and several years' experience as a Programmer
Aptitudes: Excellent communications skills
Salary Range: $25,000 to $60,000 per year

The Systems Analyst is the architect of the computer team. It is his job to design the systems that will store, process, and report the information that is the lifeblood of his company. A good Analyst must have a thorough knowledge of business procedures and a detailed knowledge of his own company's business. A solid grounding in accounting principles is also useful, for he will frequently design computer reports that will pass before the accountant's watchful eye.

The Analyst must wear two hats. He must be able to talk the technical language of programming so that he can convey his concepts to the Programmer, and he must also be able to talk the language of business to those people in the company who need computer services even if they don't know the first thing about computers. Most good Systems Analysts have come up through the ranks and have spent five or more years as Programmers. They have a thorough understanding of what a computer can and cannot do.

The Systems Analyst's work can be divided into three main groupings: file design, systems design, and program design. It is the Analyst who must decide if the latest database and online techniques would be beneficial to his company, so the successful Systems Analyst must keep in touch with the latest developments in computer technology.

The Systems Analyst is the key person on the data processing team. If the system has not been designed correctly in the first place, nothing the Programmer or Computer Operator can do will save it.

Position: Director of Data Processing
Educational Requirements: MBA frequently required
Aptitudes: Must be strong in management skills, communication, and decision-making
Salary Range: $40,000 to $100,000

The Director of Data Processing is a manager of managers—in this case the Managers of Systems and Programming, Operations, and Technical Support. He is a highly paid person who has been in the field for many years and has a great deal of authority and responsibility within his company. While he may inspire respect or even fear in his staff, remember that he has ultimate responsibility for the performance of the entire data processing department and for the jobs and well-being of up to two hundred people.

He is responsible for planning, organizing, and directing the work of his department. He is involved in the hiring of all employees and in the evaluation process for all promotions. In most companies he is in the somewhat frustrating position of being responsible for the work, but not actually taking part in it. In smaller companies he may be a "shirt-sleeves" or "working" manager who pitches in on the system design and even on occasion solves some complex programming problem after everyone else has given up.

But in the main his day is filled with administrative paperwork, meetings with upper-echelon managers, and the formulation of crucial decisions that may well spell success or failure for the entire data processing team.

SAMPLE RÉSUMÉ
JOHN DATA

46-16 65th Place   36 years old
Woodside, N.Y. 11377   Married
(212) 555-1177   Health—Excellent
                Present Position—Systems Analyst
                Present Salary—30.1K

EDUCATION:
City College of New York, August 1979, Bachelor of Arts
New York University, July 1984, Graduate studies in
    systems and programming
IBM, April 1987, CICS/VS Workshop, ALC Workshop

PROFESSIONAL EXPERIENCE:
Abraham & Straus
420 Fulton Street
Brooklyn, N.Y.
My strength is in the analysis, design, and implementation
of systems to satisfy a user's real needs. In my present position
with a major department store chain, where I have been
employed since August 1986, I have attained a position of
complete responsibility for the existing Payroll/Personnel
System, which pays over 10,000 employees on a weekly basis.
My current staff consists of six programmers. Additional
areas of expertise include On Line System design under
CICS, Point of Sale System design, and large-scale project
control. Systems were implemented in COBOL and BAL, to
run on a 370/158 (VS).

Incentive Systems, Inc.
355 Lexington Avenue
New York, N.Y.
At ISI, where I was employed from February 1984 to June
1986, I designed and implemented several major daily pro-

duction systems, both in the areas of batch processing and MIS. These were the Dues System, which records and reports dues information on 100,000 union members, the Newpac System, which issues the correct ID cards to new union members, and the Check Reconciliation System, which issues and controls benefit checks and updates the statistical and financial files. Systems were implemented in COBOL, BAL, and RPG II to run on a 360/40.

Time, Inc.
Time-Life Building
New York, N.Y.
At Time, Inc., where I was employed from June 1983 to February 1984, I became expert in index-sequential files for Disk, using random access techniques, and wrote several major COBOL programs using these disk techniques. I also used the Core Resident Cylinder Index, which increases random disk speed by as much as 50%. I wrote one major masterfile update and edit, which required 100K, tested each input record for up to 99 possible edit errors, and was the largest program in production at Time, Inc.

Great American Insurance Co.
99 John Street
New York, N.Y.
At this company, where I was employed from September 1979 to May 1983, I first took part in six months of extensive in-hours training by IBM instructors, and put this training to use in the conversion of a Major Autocoder System into COBOL to run on a 360/65 OS (MVT). Following this, I specialized in the design and writing of edit-programs. I wrote the entire front end for the Premium Entry System, which consisted of six major edits and updates.

REFERENCES: Will be furnished upon request.

Writing Your Résumé

It is difficult, if not impossible, to get a good job in data processing without a well-written résumé. At every interview you have during your career, the interviewer will first ask for your résumé. By reading this one page he can quickly get an idea of your education and experience. It will help him decide if you fit the needs of his department and give him a convenient opening to start the interview.

The format of a résumé is fairly standard, but the impression it gives of your capabilities is up to you. The accompanying sample was prepared by a professional résumé service, and the neat border and quality printing help to enhance the impression of competence. At the top, in the center, type your name in capital letters. To the left enter your full address and phone number where you can be easily reached. The purpose of a résumé is to get that all-important first interview, so it is essential that the person reading it be able to reach you easily. To the right enter your age and marital status.

In the center, below this information, enter the position desired. If this will be your first job in data processing, don't put down "Manager of Systems and Programming" even if that your ultimate goal. For a first job, the titles Data Control Clerk, Programmer Trainee, Junior Programmer, Computer Operator, or Operator Trainee are more appropriate. If you are seeking one of these positions, do not enter salary desired. Salaries for these entry-level spots are fairly standard, and you probably will get a little more than you would have specified by waiting for an offer at the interview. Instead, type the words "SALARY DESIRED— Open." If you are currently in the field and planning to change positions, give your current salary, with thousands represented by the letter K. For example, Present Salary—27.5K means $27,500 per year.

Next, in the left-hand margin type the word EDUCATION followed by a brief summary of your educational background. Follow this with PROFESSIONAL EXPERIENCE in the left-hand margin and write a paragraph about each of the jobs you've had in data processing. These should be in reverse order, with your current position first. If you are presently working and looking for a better job, it is advisable not to include the name and address of your present employer.

Each paragraph should emphasize your responsibilities and accomplishments. If you supervised another employee or designed a system, be sure to mention it. While your résumé should be complete and accurate, it is perfectly acceptable to emphasize your accomplishments. Be sure to include the specific computer languages, operating systems, computer hardware, and types of systems—payroll, general ledger, accounts receivable—that you have worked with. The next step, the interview, is based on your résumé, so make it one you can be proud of. It is a summary of your working life.

THE INTERVIEW

In a large company, your first interview will be with Personnel, where they will ask you to fill out an application for employment and check to see that your qualifications fall within the general guidelines for the job. The first step is to get past Personnel, because they cannot hire you. The only person you should ever accept a job from is the person you are going to be working for.

If Personnel decides you are qualified, they will send you to the data processing department, where you will be interviewed by one or more managers. You may be called back for as many as three interviews before you are offered the job. The first is usually an exploratory interview, to see if there is a match between your career goals and the currently available position. The second may be a purely technical interview, to evaluate your computer skills. If you have to take a programming test, grin and bear it. The actual job offer might be made at the third interview. This is your chance to negotiate for the best possible salary and benefits and a promise of the earliest possible evaluation for a raise or promotion. Ultimately, whether or not you get a job offer from the manager who interviews you depends on two things: whether he likes you, and whether he thinks you can do the job. Your only possible goal at an interview is to get the job, so project an image of friendliness and competence. It is advisable to let the interviewer do most of the talking, only to answer direct questions, and not to volunteer information needlessly.

Larger companies usually are more careful about checking your references after you are hired. Often a major corporation will write to every employer and school listed on your résumé. A small company may simply make a phone call to your previous employer to ask a few questions. Remember that most personnel departments will not reveal your exact salary. When you are negotiating for salary, most companies realize that you are looking for an increase. This generally will fall in the range from 10 percent to 20 percent of your most recent salary. If this is your first job in data processing, a programmer trainee without a college degree can expect about $22,000 per year; a beginning computer operator, around $17,000; and a data control clerk, somewhat less. Don't be discouraged by a low starting salary, since it is not unusual for people in data processing to double their salary during the first couple of years.

When looking for a job, consider these three questions:

Do I want it?
Can I get it?
Can I keep it?

If the answer to all three is yes, then it is the job for you.

3

Programmers Are People

The first computer, the ENIAC, was a U.S. military secret, almost as though it were a weapon. Today people sometimes act as if the computer were a business weapon or a protective device. Does a computer actually protect the business that owns it? No, although a large expensive computer system may make employees **feel** secure.

Is a computer a weapon against other companies? Possibly it is, because of its incredible speed and accuracy. Can a computer help management to predict the future? Yes, more than any other device. Through techniques called simulation and model-building, a computer can project data from the past and present into the future with surprising reliability. This area of computer science is called management science, information theory, or operations research.

All programming has a psychological aspect as well as a technical aspect. Programming is, after all, a human activity. And it is this psychological aspect that often interferes with doing good data processing.

As a case in point, why are business programs so large? Programs 500 pages in length are not uncommon. One of the reasons is that in the United States, until recently, we have encouraged bigness. In the typical business environment two things are going on: data processing and empire building. Empire building is characterized by building a huge staff, purchasing the largest, newest, most expensive computer, and creating a complex bureaucracy that slows work to a crawl. Managers who are empire builders often command huge salaries and astronomical departmental budgets. Systems analysts are encouraged to design larger and larger systems. Programmers soon learn never to write one line of code when one hundred lines will do the same job just as well. As a result, the computer is soon overburdened. The manager of operations, instead of requesting a smaller programming staff writing good programs, requests an even larger computer.

COMPUTER PROGRAMS
Computer programs can be evaluated as good or bad. What makes a good computer program?

1. It works. That is, of course, the primary consideration.
2. It is fast and efficient in its utilization of computer resources. The two most important resources are memory and CPU (central processing unit) time. Other important resources are input/output devices, secondary storage such as tape or disk, and required computer operator intervention.
3. It is as simple in design and coding technique as possible while still solving the problem. Some programmers deliberately try to make their programs as complex as possible, and some of them even get away with it for a while.
4. It is well documented, so that another programmer can easily read and understand it.
5. It prints a clear audit trail, including record counts and dollar amounts of input and output,

so that it can easily be verified as correct each time it is run.

Maintaining a business program is usually harder than writing one. It involves getting into someone else's logic, and people think in very different ways. As soon as you consider programs that require some reasoning ability, you find that different programmers are able to solve the problem and get the correct output, but that their programs contain different instructions arranged in different ways. When you work on a computer program that was written by someone who thinks very differently from you, it can be extremely difficult.

Business programs bomb out or fail more often than anyone would suspect. Programmers frequently get phone calls at two o'clock in the morning asking them to drive to the computer center to do what is called a quick and dirty fix. If you were fixing a computer program at two in the morning, when you were half asleep, you would probably do a quick and dirty fix also. This means the programmer is not really getting into the problem, not really getting into the program logic in depth. He's just figuring out a way to get the program running again. He may drop a bad record from the input file, or simply code in a branch around the part of the program that bombed. His main goal is to get the program running again and go home and go back to sleep.

I can't tell you how often I've received the dread two a.m. phone call. After correcting the problem, the big choice is whether to stick around until nine and be a hero, or simply drop a note on your boss's desk and go home to sleep. As I remember it, at first I opted for the hero route, but the thrill quickly wore off. Then I would just leave a note, go home to sleep, and take the following day off. Soon I realized that the smart thing to do was to **become** a boss, so that I could receive someone else's notes.

Why do programs have to be fixed so quickly in the middle of the night? Because of the constant pressure of input data. In a high-pressure corporate environment, data is like water in a pipe: you've got to keep it flowing or you'll wind up with a flood.

Sometimes companies don't want fast and efficient programs. Why? Operations may be making a case to upper management for a larger computer. They may want to be able to say they can no longer complete the daily computer production in twenty-four hours. In that environment, if a clever programmer shows them how to make the existing programs run much faster, he may find that his efforts are not fully appreciated.

Large programming projects are very difficult to schedule. Suppose you are installing a system with eighty-five programs that have to run sequentially. You get up to step seven and the program bombs out with some kind of bug or error. It takes your best programmer four days of constant effort to solve the problem. Your boss is climbing the wall, because the entire system must be installed in a month, and four days have just been wasted on one step.

What can you say to him? Can you say that the project will get back on schedule once the problem in step seven has been solved? How can you predict the future? There may be another serious problem in step ten, step fifteen, step thirty-seven, and so on down the line. The point is that in scheduling complex, highly technical programming projects there is an element of crystal-balling. Each serious program bug discovered might be the last—or it might not be. Solving one technical problem may only lead to uncovering the next.

LEARNING TO PROGRAM

How can we study programming? Programming is a rich and complex activity, difficult to learn and difficult to teach. It seems that students fall into two groups, those who "get it" and those who don't. We say that those who "get it" have a logical mind. As far as math and programming go, they can take care of themselves. But what can we do for those who don't "get it"?

1. Provide many simple examples in a beginner's language such as BASIC (Beginners' All-purpose Symbolic Instruction Code).
2. Give plenty of opportunity to run these programs over and over on a computer until they work.
3. Provide constantly available consultants to help them debug their programs. Let them talk to several consultants: If they don't understand one, maybe they will understand another.
4. Make sure of the easy availability of well-written textbooks and reference books.
5. If all else fails, CAI may work. CAI is Computer Assisted Instruction, in which a computer modifies the pace and sequence of a lesson based on interaction with the student.

There is a great difficulty in predicting programming ability. Recently I hired a young programmer who scored 95 percent on the COBOL test I give to everyone I interview. He did well for about a week and then came to me and said, "I'm not sure this is working out." When I asked what the problem was, he complained that the work was too difficult. I told him that this was programming, that if he couldn't do it here, he couldn't do it anywhere. He had just finished applying some detailed modifications to a complex COBOL program, and he seemed nervous about testing the modified code. At my urging, he finally ran one test on the computer, got some error messages, and promptly resigned. A few days later I tested his program in a slightly different way, and it worked perfectly. Not a line of code had to be changed. This experience gave me some second thoughts about my COBOL test. Obviously, it was accurately predicting programming ability but not evaluating the personality factors required to succeed in a pressured business environment.

The best way to learn is by doing. Still, many programmers consider it a mark of status to be sent to IBM for expensive technical courses. The problem arises when a programmer returns from one of those courses and isn't immediately given that kind of work to do. The courses are usually so specific and so full of detailed programming techniques that the newly acquired skills are very easily forgotten if not immediately put to use. It is important to schedule programming courses so that when the employee returns to his job, he will actually be doing what he has learned.

Data processing courses come in three flavors: too hard, too easy, and just right. Some material is too difficult and goes over the student's head. Some material is too easy or merely rehashes what the student already knows. And some material is just right: new but comprehensible. This is information that the student can add to his fund of knowledge.

On the Job

The programmer does not work in isolation. He works as a member of a complex social environment, and his social skills may be as important as his technical skills in determining his ultimate success or failure.

Important environmental factors include:

1. Freedom from excessive noise and interruption.
2. Availability of programming tools.
3. Access to the computer on a reliable basis with reasonable turnaround time, or even better, access to a computer terminal.
4. Reasonable levels of ongoing communication and cooperation with other members of the programming group.
5. Motivation to do his best, including a good salary, opportunity for advancement, opportunities to learn new skills, and intellectually challenging work.

There is another element, and that is the importance of being accepted by the group. Independent consultants are frequently evaluated purely on the basis of their work, but at most companies there is a very strong social clique in the data processing department, and you either fit in or you don't. On a new job, you will find out within a few weeks if you have been accepted as a member of the group. Do people come over and talk to you during coffee break? Has anyone asked you to have lunch? Do you feel comfortable? On a new job, having just one person you can relate to makes all the difference in the world.

Although acceptance is often found in social groups at work, within those groups there can be competition. For example, some members compete for a nice quiet office. Often programmers must work in noisy cubicles, making it difficult to concentrate; so when an office becomes available they each scramble to get it.

There are good and bad techniques of competition. Some of the bad techniques are deliberately withholding information, monopolizing computer time, and unethical acts such as discarding another programmer's listing. These things happen more frequently than anyone would suspect. Some of the good techniques include doing your best work, working long hours, studying computer manuals at home, and becoming known as an expert in some specific programming technique. In the final analysis, cooperation can be more productive than competition, and the project leader who can foster a spirit of cooperation in his programming team is probably on the right track.

THE PROGRAMMING TEAM

The programming team is usually made up of these four types of employees, each of whom must have different skills and aptitudes:

1. The project leader. Most important are the ability to foster a team spirit and to motivate a staff strongly.
2. The systems analyst. Most important are good communication skills and creative approaches to problem-solving.
3. The programmer. Most important are technical skills and knowledge of the computer.
4. The programmer-trainee. Most important are the ability to be quiet, to learn quickly and systematically, and to handle without complaint, as the price of apprenticeship, the vast amount of clerical work that every programming project generates.

Every programming team has a project leader or manager, who is responsible for the entire programming project. His functions include planning, organizing, staffing, directing, controlling, and recording and evaluating the progress of each employee as well as the ongoing progress of the entire project. The project leader who gets deeply involved in a specific programming task will soon find that he is not really doing his job.

In his plan for the project, he must set a goal and then divide the plan into logical phases to achieve that goal. He must organize a team structure of analysts and programmers, and interview and hire talented staff members. He must create an environment conducive to productivity, with the necessary programming tools and computer resources. He must direct his staff in the performance of the planned activity and control their progress toward the goal. Finally, usually using some kind of scheduling tool such as a Pert Chart or Gannt Chart, he must record their hours and evaluate their performance. On the basis of this evaluation, he can modify the plan, the staff, the goal, or the environment as required.

Less than half of all computer projects reach a successful conclusion. Of those that are completed, few go into production on schedule. Most target dates are unrealistic. Because of the difficulty of predicting technical problems and change, it is tacitly acknowledged in the industry that accurate scheduling of major projects is virtually impossible, and target dates are set to get the ball rolling. Computer projects take a long time, much longer than anyone would guess. Typically, a target date is set six months or a year in the future just to get things moving. As the deadline approaches and it is clear that more time is required, the target date is moved forward. Schedules tend to become more accurate after work is under way, since the time taken to complete the initial tasks can be used as a measure to judge the time required for the remaining phases of the project. During the life cycle of the average project, the schedule may be modified five or six times.

There are three levels of management: upper management, middle management, and line management. An upper manager such as a president or vice president is responsible for strategic management and sets long-term goals for his company in a five-year plan. A middle manager such as a director or departmental manager engages in tactical management and sets goals for his department in a one-year plan. A line manager such as a project leader is expected to provide operational management and sets day-to-day goals to solve current problems.

The Peter Principle, set forth in a humorous manner by a very clever business writer, states that employees tend to rise to their own level of incompetence. The theory is that when employees succeed in a difficult job, they get one more promotion to a job they can't quite handle, and they remain in that position for the remainder of their career. There is more than a grain of truth in this.

In 1969 the second North Atlantic Treaty Organization Conference on Data Processing was held, and the emphasis was already very different from that of the conference held the previous year. The focus was now on people as opposed to computers. This quotation from the proceedings will help to illustrate the problem:

"We made a study of about a dozen projects, though not in a very formal manner. However, our results were convincing enough to us to set up a course on programming systems management.

"The nature of the study was 'Why do our projects succeed or fail?' We took as successful a project that met its requirements on schedule within the budgeted dollars and satisfied the customer. On that basis, out of ten or twelve projects that we examined, we had one success and a whole lot of failures.

"We analyzed the reasons for failure, as given to

us by people who had performed previous evaluations of the projects. They gave various reasons behind the failure of the projects, virtually all of which were essentially management failures. We ran into problems because we didn't know how to manage what we had, not because we lacked the techniques themselves."

However, not everyone agreed with this conclusion. An alternate point of view was expressed on the second day of the conference:

"Basically all problems are technical. If you know what you want to do and you have the necessary technical background, there is no point in making a great management problem out of it. Obviously a certain amount of resource control and personnel work have to go on, but that's all."

Here are some of the reasons that programming projects fail:

1. Turnover in personnel. Programmers are in very strong demand. As their experience increases, it is often difficult for a company to continue to increase salaries to their true market worth. One wit has branded programmers "technological fruit tramps."
2. Vague and constantly changing specifications; users sometimes don't know what they want from the computer.
3. Major unplanned changes in hardware or software environment.
4. Impossibly overcrowded or noisy work environment.

5. A manager who encourages destructive competition.
6. An unrealistic and inflexible schedule.
7. Overwhelming and unnecessary complexity.
8. Lack of communication between members of the project team.

The truth of the matter, of course, is that both technical and human resources are of great importance in every programming project.

Not all programming is the same. Classroom exercises are very different from professional business programs. The most obvious difference is size and complexity. A classroom exercise might be one page long, while a major COBOL program at a large corporation might run 500 pages. However, it is important to realize that the classroom exercise took an hour or two to complete, whereas the 500-page business program might have taken a year.

PROGRAMMING APTITUDES

Professional programs can be grouped into several main types, and different programming aptitudes are required for each type:

1. Business programs are usually written in COBOL and require some knowledge of accepted business and accounting practices as well as technical skill.
2. Scientific programs are usually written in FORTRAN and require strong mathematical skills up to the level of calculus and analysis.
3. System programs (also called software programs) are usually written in Assembly language and require a detailed knowledge of computer internals.

4. Microcode (or Firmware) is written in machine language for dedicated microprocessors and requires strong engineering skills.

The type of person who would make a good software programmer would probably not be a good team leader or systems analyst. Different skills and personality traits are required. The team leader must motivate and plan. The systems analyst must deal with users and create a system to be accepted and used by them. And the systems programmer, the scientist on the programming team, must solve highly complex technical problems.

The personality fit or mesh of the various members of the programming team is far more important than is conventionally realized. Serious personality clashes have been the root cause of the failure of all too many programming projects. As we have discussed, different members of the programming team need different personality strengths. In addition, various phases of the programming task can be directly associated with critical personality factors.

Intelligence and reasoning ability are required to accomplish complex coding. A suspicious nature is useful for debugging or finding the errors in a program, but a certain amount of trust is required for working with other members of the programming team. Patience is required when dealing with users who have little knowledge of data processing, but dominance is a useful trait when dealing with computer operators. Emotional stability is required of programmers working on a tight schedule, whereas consultants who move from project to project must be adaptable to sudden change. In all cases, a certain amount of assertiveness is required simply to get work done.

Good programmers are made, not born, but certain factors are more common in successful programmers than in the general population. These include high intelligence and problem-solving ability, abstract reasoning ability, and attention to detail. Good programmers have the ability to work very hard for short periods of time and to focus all their mental resources on the task at hand. Professional programmers have excellent work habits, especially the ability to divide a major task into efficient subtasks. Both analysts and programmers must have excellent communication and language skills.

Many attempts have been made to design tests that will accurately predict programming ability, with only limited success. A notable example is the Brandon Exam, which is an eight-hour test of logical ability, and it certainly at least verifies a person's willingness to engage in programming activities for eight hours in a row. IBM has devised an exam called the PAT or Programmers Aptitude Test; it has been used so widely that it is probably overexposed by now, with sample tests and answers available in several publications. A psychologist named Mayer came up with what is known as Mayer's X-Factor. The X-Factor is measured by casually asking, "Do you like programming?" during the course of an interview. A strongly affirmative answer was taken as a good sign. Mayer claimed that there is no more accurate way to predict programming ability and success, and he may just be right.

Motivation, training, and experience are the three main elements in the making of a programmer. The ideal situation would be one hundred percent motivation, college-level training, and years of in-depth experience in the exact area in which the programmer is assigned to work. Needless to say, this is rarely the case. In fact, all too often an underpaid and disgruntled programmer with little training and no relevant experience is expected to carry the weight of a difficult new project in a noisy, crowded office. Equally often, a programmer finds himself severely underutilized, with little to do but read manuals or daydream and pretend to work.

Both of these situations are management failures and point up one of the main difficulties the project leader faces: feeding a steady flow of challenging work to the programmer.

To the uninitiated, motivation means high salary, training means frequent weeks away at IBM courses, and experience is equivalent to the number of years the employee has been in the field. But there are more subtle interpretations as well. Motivation can mean team spirit and interesting work. Training is often most effective when it comes on the job from a senior programmer who shows genuine involvement. And experience has an element of quality that cannot be measured by a simple count of years in the field.

For many, the real motivation is building a program that works, and programming on a readily available computer is still the best teacher of all.

What would your attitude be if a professor told you that no matter how hard you studied for his course you were going to get a D? You would probably feel discouraged, and you almost certainly wouldn't study very hard. It's important for most people to know that if they do well they will be rewarded. It's important to know the next rung on the ladder and that you at least have a chance of reaching it. When you are trying to achieve a promotion, it tends to make you work harder.

COMPUTER LANGUAGES

The ideal language for a computer is machine language. This is the only language a computer understands, and in fact, all early programming was done in machine language. Well-written machine language produces the fastest, most efficient programs. Unfortunately, machine language is extremely difficult to write, modify, document, or maintain. Instead, today we write programs in high-level languages that are compiled into machine language by a program supplied by the computer manufacturer. The most popular—COBOL, FORTRAN, and BASIC—are English language–based. Even programming in Assembly language, which is midway between machine language and the high-level languages, is becoming a lost art.

Programming is a form of communication between two different types of intelligence, man and machine. High-level languages and all the associated compilers and interpreters are there to aid one of them. Which one? Certainly not the computer, for no computer ever printed a message to the operator complaining that machine language was too difficult to understand.

Nevertheless, we may find our means of communication becoming more logical and less emotional (or even less human) to fit the brave new world of the computer.

And why not? Hasn't every other major technical innovation changed the way we behave?

Look at how some other inventions significantly changed our lives. The printing press and the book virtually made knowledge possible and efficiently allowed it to be passed from generation to generation. The electric light allowed us to control our day and decide when we would go to sleep. Television and radio are the most powerful means of mass communication on earth today, and video recorders allow us to personalize this power. The pocket calculator radically changed the ability of the average person to do complex math. As a result, some students have lost the ability to do multiplication and division, and some teachers ban calculators from their classrooms for that very reason. The telephone, obviously, has radically changed the way we communicate with one another. The automobile and airplane have made the world a smaller place. Finally, the computer has become a powerful tool for turning the overabundance of raw data in the world around us into usable information.

All of this, and especially the personal home computer, is leading to what is called the Wired Nation, where we will all be able to communicate instantly with a gigantic central databank. One communication expert has called the modern world a Global Village, where we communicate as easily with people on the other side of the planet as our ancestors did with members of their own village.

On the cover of the book *Programming Languages: History and Fundamentals* by Jean Sammets is a picture of the Tower of Babel. This is an appropriate image, for the book's index lists 117 computer languages. Early languages focused on the machine's requirements, but more recent languages focus on the needs of the programmer. Some recent report writer languages, oversimplified until they have lost essential flexibility, are advertised with the claim that any business executive can learn to use them, but acceptance of these User Languages has been slow.

More important has been the development of interactive languages for the experienced programmer, which allow him to communicate on an online real-time two-way basis with the computer. One of these, IBM's TSO or Time Sharing Option, even allows the programmer to stop his program during a test, look inside it to examine the various registers and the contents of data items, perhaps even change the value contained in one of these, and then command the computer to resume the test. Another Editor from IBM, ICCF (Interactive Computing and Control Facility), allows the programmer to split the CRT screen and view two computer programs simultaneously.

The desire for simpler and more powerful programming tools has led to extremely complex software "behind the scenes," and this in turn has led to the routine acceptance of gigantic memories for ordinary business computers. A megabyte of memory means one million characters of primary storage. Twenty years ago, 128,000 characters was considered a sizable memory, but small business computers are now routinely delivered with sixteen megabytes. Secondary storage devices frequently accommodate a gigabyte—one billion characters of storage!

The rapid development of new programming languages has led to inevitable problems. When a manufacturer develops a new programming language, he tests it at least twice before offering it for sale as a new software product. The first test is called the Alpha Site Test and is conducted privately at the manufacturer's own computer center. After the software has been substantially debugged, it is ready for the Beta Site Test, which is conducted out in the real world at the computer center of a major customer like Citibank or General Motors. McDonnell Douglas Aircraft, for example, was the Beta Site for IMS (Information Management System), the most powerful operating system available.

The rapid development of new software has led to what might be called the Inadvertent Beta Site, a customer who has innocently purchased what he thought was a finished software product, only to find himself assisting the manufacturer in the final stages of debugging. Undoubtedly, the manufacturer is very responsive, providing the best technicians and often a twenty-four-hour hotline to help the customer with his unexpected and often very expensive problems. The trouble is that the Inadvertent Beta Site is sometimes a small company that cannot afford the delays and disruption inherent in trying to work with what is essentially an unfinished software product. The small company has three choices. It can continue to assist the manufacturer, it can abandon the new software and restart its programming project using an older and more proven programming tool, or it can sue the manufacturer. None of these is very much fun, and the old maxim "Let the buyer beware" is probably most applicable.

There are many other programming tools besides computer languages, compilers, interpreters, and interactive online editors. Librarian software helps us store, retrieve, and modify our programs. Data generators help us test them efficiently. Autoflow software automatically draws logic flowcharts from source code and relieves some of the tedium of documentation. Word processing software helps in the preparation of all kinds of printed text. Utility programs and sorts come precoded to perform many common functions.

Nevertheless, systems are complex, sometimes much more complex than warranted by the work they do. A system is not just application programs, software, hardware, and printed output reports. The attitude and involvement of the user are a critical part of the system. The most technically perfect computer system will be a failure if the user does not accept it as a valuable tool.

It is time to expose the programming myths that have become almost a matter of tradition and get on with the real work at the heart of the complexity. That real work is doing good data processing.

FIVE PROGRAMMING MYTHS

1. The small error. There are no small errors in data processing. It is the only field where the omission of a single hyphen can cost a company $18 million. This was an actual event. An $18 million rocket was destroyed because of the

omission of a single hyphen in the computer program that launched it.

2. Men are better programmers than women, because they are more math minded and more mechanically inclined than women. This has been proven completely false. Data processing is more open to women and minority-group members than almost any other profession.

3. A programmer who has not advanced into management after five years with one employer should look for another job. This is absolutely false. Some people are cut out to be programmers, and some people are cut out to manage programmers. If a person really enjoys programming, he should stick with it. A recent ad offered $50,000 a year for an experienced CICS Systems Programmer. A thousand dollars a week is more than many managers earn, and the ad clearly indicates that there is no reason for a person who excels at technical work to move into an area fraught with people-problems, heavy responsibility and pressure, and often cutthroat office politics.

4. It is possible for an experienced manager to devise a detailed schedule for a complex project and make his programmers stick to it. This is false because of the concept of unrevealed levels of technical difficulty. Debugging a major program is somewhat like peeling an onion: each layer of technical difficulty removed reveals a new one beneath it.

5. Programmers will become obsolete as computers get more intelligent. This is absolutely false. As computers get more intelligent, it is because more intelligent software has been written by

more intelligent programmers. The intelligence of a computer is completely man-made.

THE FALSE MYSTIQUE

In the early days of computing, programmers coded entirely in machine language. Programming was part science, part arcane art. The businessmen who hired the programmers were totally mystified and thus were willing to pay exorbitant salaries and enormous prices for the computers. Programmers formed an unofficial priesthood and maintained it by making their programs and systems so large and complex that only they could understand them.

IBM was the false god this priesthood worshipped, and it was in IBM's financial interest to maintain the false mystique surrounding data processing. If programmers wrote incredibly long programs, IBM would be able to sell incredibly large computers for astronomical prices.

Although the mystique is still in force, the worship of bigness peaked in the seventies with IBM's introduction of CICS—the Customer Information Control System—the largest and most complex online monitor ever sold to a gullible business world. The minicomputer and microcomputer revolution helped to burst the bubble when businessmen found out what small and efficient computers could do.

Today the priesthood continues to worship its false god, but more and more businessmen have noticed that Emperor IBM isn't wearing any clothes. However, whenever businessmen have the chance to spend money that isn't their own on high technology they don't quite understand, the price will be very high.

THE PARABLE OF THE ZEN MONKS

Long ago in the distant past, in a magical kingdom by

the sea, the people lived by trading seashells. One apple was worth three shells, a pork chop was priced at forty seashells, and a donkey cost two hundred seashells. A small house cost about forty thousand seashells, and it took a lot of counting to buy a house, since all of the counting was done by hand. Living together in the magical kingdom in a run-down monastery was a group of Zen monks who didn't have anything to do but tend a small vegetable garden and sit in the sun. They were very poor and sometimes went hungry.

One day the youngest monk said, "Let's become Counters! When someone wants to buy a house, we'll count the forty thousand seashells and keep five of them for our trouble, and then we'll be able to buy some meat to go with the vegetables from our garden."

All the other Zen monks agreed, and they started practicing their counting with pebbles from the garden. At first business was slow, but after they had accurately counted out eighty thousand shells in record time for a miller who was buying a luxurious mansion, people began to compete for their services. They were even able to raise their rates until they kept one out of every hundred seashells they counted. They divided up the profits, and soon each monk was making thirty thousand shells a year.

Time rolled on in the magical kingdom by the sea, and the day came when only the monks remembered how to count shells. Everyone else had forgotten how. The monks were each making sixty thousand shells per year, and now they had wine to go with the meat to go with the vegetables from their garden. Everyone but the monks believed that counting shells was an impossibly difficult and mystical process and that only a monk could ever do it correctly.

Time continued to roll by as it does even in magical kingdoms, and the monks were gaining more and more

51

power. One day they woke up to find they were the rulers of the magical kingdom by the sea, and they promptly moved into a huge castle with a very well-stocked vegetable garden.

Sometimes people talked about counting, but only in small groups, and only in whispers. Everyone agreed it was something that only monks could do, and soon even the whispers stopped.

Moral: Learn how to count, and keep it a secret.

4

Hardware: From Minis to Supercomputers

It is safe to say that all of us have used a pocket calculator at one time or another. Calculators and microcomputers are very much alike today. In fact, both are
manufactured using the same type of microprocessor
integrated circuit, and several brands of pocket
computer—about the same size as a calculator—are
gaining in popularity. The big difference is that the
computer can store and execute a program.

Calculators made the changeover from mechanical to
electronic as recently as 1964. The first all-electronic
calculator was manufactured by Friden in that year,
and it sold for over $2,000. Today a quality electronic
pocket calculator with similar functions costs about $20.
In 1971 the Mostek Corporation developed the first
calculator on a chip. This meant that instead of using
many transistors to build a calculator, these components
were further miniaturized and placed on a single integrated circuit. The calculator chip quickly went from
an original price of $400 to under $15 each through
the amazing efficiencies of mass production. This led
directly to the pocket calculator craze of the seventies.

Today the same efficiency is applied to the manu-
facture of small computers. The development of the
integrated circuit led to the production of the micro-

processor, often called a "computer on a chip." With this development, the size and price of computers shrank dramatically, allowing for mass production.

There are four main types of calculators: the standard four-function model, the expanded model, the scientific model, and the programmable model. The standard model does only simple calculations: addition, subtraction, multiplication, and division. It is, however, a useful tool for the student. The expanded model adds the percent key and a limited amount of memory. The scientific calculator adds log, sine, cosine, and other special-purpose keys for advanced math. The programmable model is, of course, really a pocket computer and has sufficient memory to retain the steps for a complex series of calculations and repeat them on demand using new data. They are often programmable in the BASIC computer language. Popular models are made by Hewlett-Packard and Texas Instruments.

What are the main differences between calculators and small computers? First of all, the small computer usually has a full typewriter-style keyboard for input and displays twenty-four lines of eighty characters on a standard TV for output. The typical calculator has a small numeric keypad for data entry and only a single row of liquid crystal characters for output of a single calculated result. Computers can process letters, words, special characters, and numbers. Calculators are limited to numbers. Finally, even a small computer has much more internal memory than a calculator.

The smallest true computer is called a microcomputer. All of the home computers, including the Macintosh, IBM PS/1, and Tandy 1,000 and the wide variety of other models, are microcomputers. Laptop computers are another variety. A laptop is a portable computer that weighs eight to fifteen pounds. Other varieties of portable computers include the transportable, the ultralight, and the palmtop, which weighs less than two pounds and can be held in one hand.

Most of these, except the palmtop, which usually does not have a standard keyboard, look like typewriters, and they all use a screen for output. Substantial differences do exist, however; it is wise to try several at a computer store before choosing one. IBM and IBM-compatible computers are the most popular, but the Macintosh is liked by those interested in using graphics programs for things like desktop publishing. You must choose which will best suit your needs.

Most of the home personal computers offer peripheral devices that can be purchased later and easily attached to your machine. These peripherals include printers, disk storage devices, and cassette tape storage devices. Preprogrammed cartridges ranging from games such as Space Invaders to personal finance and word processing are widely available for home computers.

Desk-top microcomputers are becoming increasingly common in the business world. In fact, an unusual phenomenon is developing: Very similar hardware is often sold to the home computer hobbyist at one price and to a business at a much higher price.

Minicomputers are the next step up from micros in size and processing power. They are not intended for home use. One successful model is IBM's AS/400. IBM has built a $14 billion business in minicomputers, which is still growing despite heavy competition from personal computers and engineering workstations.

Minicomputers are used in three main ways in the corporate environment. They can be used as front-end data entry devices for large mainframe computers. They can be used as stand-alone self-contained computers for local financial processing. Or they can be used for special purposes ranging from scientific applications to word processing to message switching.

Minicomputers, also called medium-sized computers or midrange systems, sell for between $25,000 and $750,000. Medium-sized computers are powerful enough to handle all the financial data processing for a small to medium-sized company. The minicomputer industry has had stiff competition from personal computers during recent years. Many companies have found that a souped-up PC will serve their needs as well as a $100,000 minicomputer. Many companies, like Digital Equipment Corp., the second-biggest supplier of midrange computers, are branching out into more lucrative areas. However, IBM, which dominates this market, is preparing to release a new minicomputer model, and Data General has had much success with its Aviion line.

Large-scale computers represent the next step up in processing power. They execute instructions at a faster rate and can run many programs at the same time in separate partitions. They are often equipped with gigantic internal memories, measured in megs (millions of characters). They are used for weather forecasting, large financial applications, and military applications. Banks, insurance companies, and airlines are typical users. A large-scale computer room with dozens of tape-drives and printers all working at once can be an awesome demonstration of the power of our advanced technology. IBM's popular large-scale computers, which are also called mainframe computers, sell for between $70,500 and $22.8 million.

Supercomputers are the most powerful computers made anywhere in the world. They are used almost exclusively by the U.S. government for weather forecasting and large "number-crunching" scientific applications. Cray Research is an industry leader in the area of supercomputers. Cray's machines have the world's largest memories—up to 32 gigabytes. They are regarded as quality tools for solving challenging scientific and industrial problems. These supercomputers are custom manufactured and cost millions of dollars.

What kind of computers will you work with when you graduate and begin your career? An enormous amount of research and development is occurring in the computer field. The general trend is to greater miniaturization and lower cost. In the future, we can expect to see faster and more powerful computers in every category, from microcomputer to supercomputer.

A Typical Computer Room

Now that you have an idea of the wide variety of computers available, let's take a tour of a modern medium-sized computer installation. When you walk into a typical computer room, you are pleasantly surprised, since most of them are very attractive. The temperature, lighting, and security of the computer room are all carefully controlled. There is often a special lock on the door that will admit only people with authorized access. Inside, you see the computer console itself, covered with dials, lights, and switches. This is where the computer console operator sits to initiate and control the execution of programs.

Devices in the computer room are classified as input or output devices. You may first notice the large high-speed printers, since they are somewhat noisy. They are output devices, typically used for printing financial reports, payroll checks, or even computer programs. Next you may notice the large tape-drives, which are input/output devices and store data magnetically, in much the way your home cassette recorder stores music. Most computer installations use thousands of reels of tape to store the master files that record the financial history of the company. This often requires a special room, called the tape library, and a tape librarian to keep track of the many reels. Data are stored on tape sequentially, meaning that if the computer is required to access some data near the end of the tape, it must read through all the prior information first.

Disks are also input/output devices. There are more than a dozen disk-drives in a typical computer room. Like tape, they are also a magnetic medium, but on disk the data can be retrieved by direct access, meaning that a particular record can be retrieved immediately, without reading any other records. This can lead to very fast and efficient processing. For example, when you use the bank's ATM to obtain information on your current account balance, the data is retrieved from a disk using the direct access method.

Another important device is the card reader/punch. This is an input/output device used to read data from the familiar eighty-column computer card or to punch data into blank cards. At one time the punched card was the most popular medium for entering both programs and data into the computer, but in recent years the CRT (cathode-ray tube) has been gaining in popularity. The CRT is like a TV screen attached to a typewriter keyboard. It is silent and can interactively communicate with the computer. It can process data in the online real-time mode, which is fast and very efficient. For these reasons, the CRT is rapidly becoming the preferred choice for entry of both programs and data.

What you wouldn't notice during our computer room tour are the internal electronic components that actually make the computer work. There are three main internal components: the arithmetic/logic unit, the control unit, and the primary storage unit.

The arithmetic/logic unit handles the functions of addition, subtraction, multiplication, division, comparing data, and making decisions. The control unit oversees the coordinated functioning of the various parts of the computer and the input/output devices.

The primary storage unit is the memory used to hold data while it is being processed. Together, these three components make up the CPU, or central processing unit.

The various parts of the computer perform together under the control of the operating system in a complex and incredibly fast choreography. The result is such fast and accurate data processing that no large corporation could continue to function without its computer center. It is the interaction of hardware and software that makes it all possible.

5

Software: Developing a Computer Program

A computer without software is as useless as a stereo system without tapes. Software is a broad category that includes all the programs that allow a computer to do useful work. Software is divided into two large categories: system software and application software. System software is usually supplied with the computer by the manufacturer and includes the operating system, the language compilers, and the utility programs such as sorts and file utilities.

This chapter focuses on application software, which can be defined as the programs written in-house to perform useful work on the computer. Examples of this type of software are Payroll, General Ledger, Inventory, Accounts Payable, and Accounts Receivable.

The basic concept of every computer program can be summed up in three words: input, processing, and output. This means that the program reads the data input, performs calculations or other operation on it, and reports the result in a readable form. This is very similar to the way people handle information. Consider what happens when you play cards. You look at your hand to get the information about the cards dealt to you (input). You think about what card to play (processing).

Finally, you play a card (output). In an executing program, this three-phase cycle occurs over and over at lightning speed.

During the input phase the computer reads some data. The data might be a single number (called a field) or a collection of related fields (called a record). The input to a typical financial computer program is often very high volume, ranging up into the millions of records. Each one of these records must separately go through the input, processing, and output phases. That is one reason why the high-speed processing capability of the modern computer is so important.

During the processing phase, the operations the program can carry out on the data records include sorting, selecting, summarizing, performing calculations, counting, deciding, and editing. **Sorting** is putting the records into sequence on some key field; sorting can be performed on a numeric field, such as social security number, or on an alphabetic field, such as employee name. **Selecting** is choosing only some of the data records as candidates for processing. An example would be selecting all employees of an age over sixty-five, or all students with a grade point average over 3.5. **Summarizing** is frequently performed to turn vast quantities of raw data into meaningful information useful to corporate managers. Millions of sales detail records, for example, could be counted and totaled by category and presented to management as a one-page Sales Summary Report.

Performing calculations and **counting** include the almost unlimited arithmetic capability of a modern computer, which can execute thousands of calculations per second. **Deciding** refers to the logical ability to compare two numbers and base further processing on the result of the comparison. Finally, **editing** refers to a program's ability to "filter out" errors in the input data.

The most common form of editing is testing to insure that a numeric field actually contains numeric data before performing calculations.

The terms **data** and **information** have very different meanings. **Data** refers to the high-volume and very detailed input records. **Information**, however, is the summarized and processed data, now in a form useful to people who need to make decisions. During the output phase, the raw data, which have now been processed, are reported as useful information, frequently in the form of a printed computer report.

The original breakthrough that made all this possible was the concept of the stored program. On the first computers, instructions were entered one at a time by the operator, in the same way we enter instructions into a calculator. But as programs became longer and more complex, this became a time-consuming and painstaking process. It was soon decided that the series of instructions making up the program should be stored in the computer's memory before any data were read. Then the computer itself would fetch one instruction at a time and perform the desired operation. This led to much more efficient processing.

At first, all programs were written in machine language, which is complex and difficult to learn. The effort to develop "people-oriented" languages led to the concept of compilation and the high-level languages such as COBOL and BASIC.

Compilation is the process of executing a manufacturer-supplied software program called the compiler. Input to the compiler is a high-level language generally written in English. Output from the compiler is the machine language that the computer requires. Today most programmers write in a high-level language such as COBOL, FORTRAN, or BASIC, using easily re-membered instructions such as READ, PRINT,

ADD, SUBTRACT, CALCULATE. They enter into a terminal the entire series of instructions making up their program and then run the appropriate language compiler. The high-level language input to the compiler is called source code. The machine language output is called object code. It is the object code that controls the computer when the program is executed.

The computer is a problem-solving tool. To use it efficiently, systems analysts and programmers go through six steps:

1. Defining the data processing problem.
2. Planning a solution to the problem as program specifications.
3. Coding the program.
4. Compiling, debugging, and testing the program.
5. Documenting the program.
6. Implementing the program in a production environment.

The systems analyst is responsible for defining a data processing problem. He often begins with a feasibility study to define the cost-effectiveness of using the computer to solve this particular problem. Once it is clear that the project is feasible and cost-justified, the analyst works with a knowledgeable person in the user department to define the system requirements. He defines the input data now available, the processing requirements, and the ultimate information need. This is called the analysis phase.

Once the analysis phase is complete, the analyst develops his own creative system solution. This is known as the design phase. It is during the design phase that the analyst plans a solution to the original problem as a set of program specifications. The working documents the analyst produces in this phase include the systems flowchart, redesigned source documents, program flowcharts, program logic narratives, report layouts, file designs, and editing rules.

The individual program flowcharts and logic narratives that make up the program specifications are then turned over to the programmer, who codes from those specifications to produce the actual programs. The programs are coded in the most suitable language. Different languages are used for different purposes:

1. COBOL stands for COmmon Business Oriented Language. The most popular language for business applications, it is especially suited to the preparation of complex business reports.
2. BASIC stands for Beginners' All-purpose Symbolic Instruction Code. It is the most popular language for introductory courses in high school and college. It is also available for most home computers.
3. FORTRAN stands for FORmula TRANslator. It is a scientific language, used largely for high-level math, scientific calculations, operations research, and computer graphics.
4. PL/1 stands for Program Language 1. It is a multipurpose language designed for solving both business and scientific problems. It incorporates many features of FORTRAN and COBOL.
5. AGOL stands for Algebraic Oriented Language. It is principally used in programming scientific problems and is a result of international co-operation to obtain a standardized algorithmic language.
6. Pascal is a highly efficient language used in both business and industry.

Some of the available programming techniques are modular, top-down, and structured programming. These are used either to decrease programming development time or to increase the readability and maintainability of the finished program.

After coding is complete, the programmer compiles, debugs, and tests the program, using sample data. He reviews his test output with the systems analyst and the user until they agree that the program is functioning correctly. After programs have been tested individually, they are grouped together in a jobstream and tested as a system. Large systems may take years to code and test, but as newer and more efficient languages are introduced, the trend is toward shorter project cycles.

Finally, the program is documented, with special attention given to the run instructions, so that the computer operator can run the program without consulting the programmer. In addition, the systems analyst often develops a control procedure, or a set of balancing rules to insure that the printed output reports are correct before they are delivered to the user.

When the documentation is complete, the program is ready to put into production. This does not mean, however, that the programmer will never work on his production program again. A set of programs or a system is a continually evolving business tool that must grow and change as the business evolves. Over half of all programming involves changes, corrections, and maintenance to production programs, and it is often the original programmer who is called upon to do this demanding work.

6

Career Profile: Interview with a Computer Consultant

Dean is a highly paid computer consultant who has been working with computers for twelve years. He is a "high tech" expert on the Hewlett-Packard line of minicomputers. He is thirty-two years old, married, and has five children. He is currently working under a high-pressure ten-week contract for a large multinational conglomerate. He earns $1,750 per week.

Q: Dean, why don't you summarize your career and describe the series of jobs that led to your current contract?
A: Well, I've had two jobs in my whole life. The first was the Air Force, where I worked with computers for about ten years, and the second was with a large consulting firm in New Jersey that specialized in the Hewlett-Packard.
Q: Did you actually program in the Air Force?
A: I enlisted to fly, but when I flunked the flight physical, I told them I wanted a job with computers—anything to do with computers.
Q: Why did you want to get into the computer field?
A: I felt it was the up-and-coming field—and it still is today. The career potential is enormous.

Q: So what kind of job did they give you?

A: Well, first I was trained in the electronic maintenance of computers. Later I learned to program in Assembly language, FORTRAN, and COBOL, and I also did some teaching.

Q: What kind of hardware were you exposed to?

A: I was programming military and financial applications on large-scale Burroughs and IBM computers.

Q: So you really learned data processing from the ground up. How long did you program in the Air Force?

A: About six years, including FORTRAN, COBOL, and Assembly.

Q: What did you do when you finally left the Air Force?

A: I conducted a job search, focusing on the New York and Colorado areas, which were the two areas I wanted to live in.

Q: What made you decide on New Jersey?

A: I got an excellent offer from a large consulting firm there, and New Jersey seems to be the data processing capital of the world.

Q: Why do you say that?

A: Well, there are an enormous number of large computer installations in New Jersey.

Q: So what kind of work did they have you doing?

A: I learned a new online language called VIEW, specifically for the Hewlett-Packard mini, and started programming for them.

Q: Did they send you to school for that?

A: No, I picked it up on my own by reading the manuals. I had six weeks to get up to speed.

Q: How do you feel about knowing so many different computer languages? Does it ever get confusing?

A: No, but sometimes when I'm working in one language I wish I had the capability of using a specific

67

instruction or technique that exists only in another language. Each one has its strengths and limitations.

Q: What was your title at the consulting firm?

A: I was hired as a systems analyst. They always seem to give high-level programmers the title of systems analyst. But the truth of the matter is I spent most of my time coding.

Q: Did they give you any formal training at all?

A: Yes, they finally sent me to Toronto for a week to learn a new online language called QUICK. I should mention that QUICK is one of a new generation of languages known as "screen printers" that allow you to put up online screens very quickly for data entry, editing, and inquiry.

Q: What happened next?

A: Well, using QUICK I got involved in this large-scale programming project for a large multinational conglomerate. I worked on the project for about a year, and then the New Jersey consulting firm went out of business.

Q: So you found yourself without a job?

A: Yes, but because the project was right in the middle of implementation and I was essential to its completion, I was hired directly by the conglomerate as an independent consultant.

Q: What are they paying you?

A: $1,750 a week.

Q: Is that unusual?

A: Maybe a little high, but experienced consultants often earn three hundred a day.

Q: What would you say are the attitudes necessary for a career as a computer consultant?

A: You need the ability to concentrate on your work. You need the ability to think very hard for short periods of time. You need to be organized, methodical, and have a logical mind. You have to be able to focus completely on your work and cut other people off—at least while you are working.

Q: Does a programmer have to be a genius?

A: Not really. If you can play chess or solve abstract problems, you will probably enjoy programming. High school geometry and college calculus are probably pretty good predicters of programming ability.

Q: What are the educational requirements?

A: Formal instruction in the language you are going to be programming in.

Q: What about a college degree?

A: Well, a degree in computer science can be a big plus nowadays. The requirements for getting into the computer field are becoming somewhat more formal.

Q: You went to college for a few years, didn't you?

A: Yes, I was a music and theater major for about three years before I went into the Air Force. I took calculus and got a B in it. I had quite a bit of math aptitude, but I still had to work hard for that grade.

A lot of college students just seem to pick the easiest majors. They drop out of pre-med because of all the memorization, or drop out of engineering because of all the math. It isn't quite clear to them that they are going to work for the rest of their lives, and that they can achieve more in the four years of college toward raising the level of their professional career than at any other time.

Q: What do you find to be the main satisfactions of computer programming?

A: It's a creative process—you are creating a program or system that didn't exist before. When you know what you're doing, there is a sense of power in controlling the computer.

There's challenge in the work, and satisfaction in viewing the completed program in action. There is also the satisfaction of problem-solving, similar to the pleasure of winning at chess.

Then, of course, there is the money, which can be quite substantial. My programming career allows me to support my family and pay the mortgage on the house. If you enjoy travel, it's easy to find in the computer field. I also enjoy helping beginning programmers learn the fine points of the language.

Q: Are there job opportunities in the field besides the obvious ones?

A: Some people regard programming as just a stepping-stone to other positions within the company, such as management. Frequently the best programmer is promoted to systems design or project leadership.

Q: How is the financial compensation compared with other fields?

A: Right now, there is a shortage of good programmers, and the salaries are good to excellent. They begin around $18,000 for a beginner without a degree, and peak at around $45,000 for a talented and experienced systems programmer. Some of the data processing magazines publish annual salary surveys, and the top salaries increase every year.

Q: How about geographic location? Can you set up shop anywhere?

A: Just about any urban center. Some of the major corporations like IBM prefer to create a campus environment for their DP center, but the employees in those rural locations sometimes feel locked in and isolated.

Q: Can you set up your own business?

A: Sure. As an independent consultant, I have my own business right now.

Q: What kind of people do best in the field?

A: Programmers tend to be introverted, but sales or management requires a more people-oriented and extroverted personality. I have seen people with majors from music to psychology succeed as programmers, but in the future we will probably see more computer science majors.

Q: What are the different areas within the field?

A: There are three large areas: business programming, scientific programming, and the new area of personal computing. Within each of these large areas you find the full spectrum of career possibilities—sales, management, programming, design.

Q: What are some of the personal qualities desirable in the computer field?

A: Intelligence, abstract reasoning, ability to work long hours. You have to be able to handle the high pressure and also occasional lulls with nothing to do. There always seems to be too much or too little work.

Q: How are opportunities for women?

A: I'd say that there is a great deal of opportunity for women in data processing—more than in most other fields.

Q: Is there anything you would like to say in summary?

A: It's been a long day.

7

Career Profile: Interview with a College Instructor

John is a full-time instructor in the Computer Science Department of a major metropolitan university. He is thirty-eight years old and has been involved in data processing for sixteen years, ever since he graduated from college. He is a bachelor and lives in the city, near the campus. He has been teaching for two years. His prior position was as a senior programmer at a large bank, and he took a substantial pay cut to return to the academic environment.

Q: John, I find it interesting that you were willing to take a $6,000 pay reduction to move from the corporate world to the academic world. What was the reason?

A: To be honest, I really didn't fit into the corporate world. It was very high-pressure, I worked very long hours, and I was getting a first-class case of job burnout.

Q: In retrospect, are you glad you made the change?

A: Very glad. I have a much more relaxed life-style now. I teach sixteen hours a week and really enjoy my contact with the students. I have more free time for personal projects, and I'm slowly working toward my graduate degree in computer science.

Q: Would you ever go back to the bank?

A: I don't think so. That nine-to-five rat race is a little

too much for me. Especially when you wind up working late almost every night.

Q: But wouldn't you have had opportunities for advancement into management at the bank?

A: I'm not really the management type. I like the technical side of programming, I like working with students, and I consider myself basically a creative person.

Anyway, there are opportunities for advancement here at the university, too. But I'm not really that ambitious. Money isn't that important to me. This summer, for example, I'm going to be a counselor at a computer camp. I'll earn $1,200 for the whole summer, but I regard it as a paid vacation.

Q: Any other big differences between teaching and the corporate world?

A: Well, I have some good friends here at the university, which was not the case at the bank.

Q: What would you say are the attitudes necessary for a career as a college instructor?

A: It helps if you're an intellectual, and also a little bit of a ham. Your basic job is lecturing to students, and if you can turn your lecture into an interesting performance, everyone benefits.

Of course, you have to be a reader and an excellent student yourself. In addition to reading the textbooks for each course, I read various current magazines and books to stay in touch with the rapid advances in the field. It's important to genuinely like and respect the subject matter.

If I didn't enjoy working with computers, I'd have a hard time generating any enthusiasm for the subject in my students.

Also, it's important to be very patient. When I first started teaching, I went much too fast and left half the class behind. You have to aim your lecture at the average student and encourage frequent questions from the class to make sure everyone understands the lecture.

Q: What educational background is needed to go into college teaching?

A: You absolutely need your bachelor's degree to start college teaching part time as an adjunct. Then you'll need a master's or PhD in computer science to become a full professor. Of course, you can continue to work on your graduate degree even after you start teaching. There's usually a big reduction in tuition if you work for the university. That's what I'm doing; I'll have my PhD in another three years.

It also helps if you've actually worked in the field, as a programmer or an analyst, for a few years. Then you have some real-life examples to add to your lectures.

Q: What are the main satisfactions of college teaching?

A: Well, it certainly isn't the money. I'd say it's creative and enjoyable work, contact with students, personal freedom, a relaxed life-style, and plenty of vacation time to pursue your own interests.

There is also considerably more job security than in the business world, especially if you are granted tenure.

Q: What is tenure?

A: Tenure is granted to full professors who have been teaching at one university for ten years (or seven years at some schools). It basically means that you cannot be dismissed, that you have your job until you decide to retire. It was originally instituted to encourage academic freedom. It's becoming increasingly difficult to get tenure nowadays. With the baby-boom generation already graduated, college enrollment has declined, and many universities are feeling a financial pinch. Because of that, more part-time adjunct lecturers are being hired at reduced salaries. Part-timers aren't eligible for tenure.

But tenure is still possible. I hope to receive it some-day myself.

Q: Are there job opportunities in the field besides the obvious ones?

A: One of the nicest benefits of college teaching is the way it leads to other things. For example, my job this summer at the computer camp came through the placement office here. I've published some articles in computer magazines that originated as a lecture to one of my classes. Perhaps someday I'll write a textbook.

Q: Is geographic location important?

A: Not really. The basic choice is between a rural and an urban campus. Good teaching jobs are rare, however, and people will often relocate to another state to join the faculty of a respected university.

Q: Can you set up your own business?

A: Well, if you are a real organizer, I suppose you could start your own trade school in the computer field, but that doesn't appeal to me at all.

Q: What are the financial rewards of teaching?

A: Salaries are not very good, compared to computer programming for business. A full-time college instructor receives about $25,000 per year. An associate professor may receive around $33,000 annually, and a tenured professor might earn the maximum, which is currently about $41,000.

Of course, if you write a successful textbook, you can make a great deal of money.

Q: Are there leads into other fields?

A: Oh sure, there are frequent opportunities for con-sulting and lecturing in the business world. Sometimes professors leave the university and return to industry full time, often when they have a family and need the additional income.

There is also the possibility of becoming chairman

of your department or of moving into university administration, although there is a lot of politics and competition involved in obtaining those positions.

Q: What type of person do you find teaching computer science?

A: Well, I've already said he's typically an intellectual and a bit of a ham. In addition, he likes to write and usually writes well. It's hard to imagine a college teacher who doesn't enjoy writing.

Q: How about opportunities for women?

A: They are excellent. About a third of the teachers here are women. Most of the tenured full professors are still men, but that is gradually changing.

Q: What advice would you give to the student who wants to become a professor?

A: Go to the best college you can get into. Devote yourself to your studies. Major in computer science, and when you graduate, go directly into graduate school. At the minimum, you must get your master's degree.

While you are working on your master's degree, you will find it comparatively easy to teach one introductory course as an adjunct. That will give you a chance to see how you like being in front of a class.

If you do like teaching, definitely make plans to get your PhD in computer science as soon as possible. For obvious reasons, degrees are very important in the academic world. Even if you don't like teaching, complete your master's. It will give you an important competitive edge when you enter the business world.

8

Career Profile: Interview with a Systems Manager

Katya is a systems manager with a major department store chain. She is thirty-one years old and has been with her current employer for five years. She is married and has one child. She is a college graduate, with a bachelor's degree in business administration.

Q: Katya, let's start at the beginning. How did you get into the computer field?
A: Well, I did pretty well in my math courses in college, and I wasn't afraid of quantitative work. When I graduated, I took an all-day exam offered by a large bank that was supposed to predict programming ability. Of the three hundred college graduates who took the exam, I scored in the top 10 percent, and they made me an offer that I accepted.
Q: What was your job with the bank?
A: I was hired as a programmer trainee. For the first year, all I really did was go to school. Classes were in-house at the bank, and we learned the technical details of programming the bank's computers.
Q: What subjects did you study?
A: We had courses in systems analysis, COBOL, Autocoder, the Operating System, and Job Control Language. You see, the bank had a lot of programs that

were written in Autocoder, an obsolete language, and we were being trained to convert them to COBOL, which is a more modern language.

Q: What happened after you completed that year of training?

A: Well, I got a certificate and we had a little graduation party, and then they put us to work converting Autocoder to COBOL.

Q: How did it go?

A: The work was very hard, but we had some experienced consultants to help us. The problem was that the programs were old and undocumented, and nobody knew exactly what they did anymore. In my second year I converted twelve large Autocoder programs to run in COBOL.

I should mention that the working conditions were very good. There had been thirty of us in the training class, all college graduates, and we became friends. In fact, that's where I met my husband. In addition, the salaries were good, we all had small offices, and the work hours were flexible. Many of us were sent to IBM for additional education in specialized subjects.

Q: What happened next?

A: The bank merged with a larger bank, and the Data Processing Center was eliminated.

Q: Did you have to find another job?

A: Yes, I did. I was unemployed for about six months, which is a very unpleasant experience. I had gone to college on the Federal Loan Guarantee Program, and I had started paying back the loan monthly. At one point I wasn't able to make the payments. I had to write them a letter explaining that I was unemployed.

Q: Then what happened?

A: I finally got a job here at the department store as a programmer/analyst.

Q: Why do you suppose they hired you?

A: Well, the main things in my favor were that I was a college graduate, I was familiar with IBM computers, and by then I was an expert COBOL programmer. Of course, I didn't know a thing about the retail business.

Q: Did they give you any formal training?

A: Nothing formal, at first. But they wouldn't let me do any work either. For the first couple of months I just sat at my desk reading manuals and documentation.

Q: What kind of work did they finally give you?

A: I was made lead maintenance programmer for their Point of Sale System.

Q: What exactly did that entail?

A: Well, this is a large department store, with eleven branches in the metropolitan area. We use a special computerized kind of cash register called a POS (Point of Sale) Register, which is connected by phone lines to our data processing center. That way, at the time of the sale, we can capture the details of what is sold, the quantity sold, and if it is a charge-account sale we also capture the customer's account number. This all happens automatically as the sale is rung up at the register.

Once all the data are received and stored on reels of magnetic tape in the computer room, the POS Processing System runs. It edits and balances the data, reduces inventory, posts to the Sales Register, and interfaces to the Credit System for later billing of charge customers. To maintain this system, I had to become familiar with over a hundred COBOL programs.

Q: How were the working conditions?

A: Terrible. You see, the POS System ran overnight, after all the stores were closed, and it had to run every night. If anything went wrong, the computer operator would call me in the middle of the night, and I would have to drive in to the computer center to solve the problem.

Q: How often did that happen?

A: About once a week. The phone would ring around two in the morning, waking my husband and me, and I'd have to drive to the computer center. It was a real strain, but I decided to stick with it. I felt I was paying my dues, and that I would finally be rewarded by the company.

Q: Is that what happened?

A: Yes, it was. After about a year I was promoted to project leader and put in charge of a major expansion of the Point of Sale System. I hired two junior programmers who handled the emergency phone calls on a rotating basis.

Q: I'm sure that was a relief.

A: It was—both for me and my husband.

Q: How long did the POS expansion project take?

A: About two years. It was very successful, and I recently received another promotion, to systems manager. I have a nice office with a window, my own secretary, and six data processing professionals report to me. My salary has almost doubled since I started at the store five years ago. I am in charge of three systems: Point of Sale, Payroll/Personnel, and the Credit System.

Q: What attitudes would you say are necessary for a career as systems manager?

A: I use the Project Team approach. Everyone on my staff is considered a member of the team. I meet with each of my employees once a week to review their progress, and on Friday we have a team meeting in the conference room. Everyone is encouraged to discuss any work problems they have.

Q: Do you still do any programming yourself?

A: Not really. I'm too busy with meetings and administration. But I still have my COBOL skills and occasionally assist one of my programmers with a coding problem.

Q: What would you say is the required educational background for your job?

A: Well, I'd say my bachelor's degree in business administration was fine when I started. Today I'd recommend a computer science degree, possibly followed by an MBA.

Q: What are the main satisfactions of your work?

A: Data processing is a service industry. We don't earn a profit for the company, but we provide a valuable service to those areas of the company that do. So my main satisfaction is helping the user departments.

I enjoy working with people, and as a manager I have frequent contact with new people. I especially enjoy interviewing potential employees.

Q: Do you do a lot of interviewing?

A: Yes, there is quite a bit of job-hopping among programmers, so we are always looking for good programmers. Personnel sends over one or two every week for a technical interview. I've devised a brief COBOL test to keep things objective.

Q: Are there job opportunities in the field besides the obvious ones?

A: The main areas here are programming, systems, operations, and technical support. There are also the clerical areas like keypunch, data control, and the tape library. The main goal of most employees is to move up to the supervisory and management positions.

Q: How is the opportunity for advancement?

A: On the average, there is only one manager for every ten employees or so, and that leads to a lot of competition for that one management slot. My goal is someday to be Vice President in charge of Corporate Data Processing—but that's a long way off.

Q: How about geographic location? Can you find a systems manager job anywhere?

A: I imagine this profession is pretty much concentrated in urban centers.

Q: Could you set up your own business in the field?

A: There are opportunities to start service bureaus or consulting firms, but you'd have to have access to quite a lot of investment capital.

Q: What are the financial rewards?

A: We pay programmers in the low twenties, analysts in the high twenties, and managers in the thirties. My boss, the manager of data processing, probably earns about $50,000 a year, which is very good money.

Q: What kind of people are in the field?

A: You'll find a full gamut, from introverted technical types to extroverted managers who like to give orders. The one thing they have in common is that they all work very hard.

Q: Are there leads into other fields?

A: Definitely. Another systems manager here recently moved into the area of general retail management. You tend to learn the retail business after a number of years and are sometimes more valuable to the organization for your management skills than for your computer skills.

Q: How about the health factor—stress, pressure, bad hours?

A: Well, there's always a certain amount of stress and pressure in the business world. You just have to keep healthy and take it. As for bad hours, that was mostly confined to my first year with the company.

Q: How about opportunities for women?

A: We're an equal opportunity employer and give equal consideration to every applicant regardless of race or sex. However, of the twenty or so systems managers, I am one of only two women.

Q: Do you have anything you would like to say in summary?

A: Only that I feel I've been very fortunate in my choice of career. I've had some difficult times, but I've worked hard and received some rewards. Now I can look forward to a stable future for my family, and to job satisfaction for myself.

9

Career Profile: Interview with a Junior Programmer

Esther is thirty-two years old, a divorced mother with two young sons. She is a graduate of Control Data Institute and has been employed as a programmer for a year and a half. She is currently with a major supermarket chain in the New York area.

Q: Esther, let's begin at the beginning. How did you get into data processing?
A: I did something I had wanted to do even before I graduated from high school: I took a crash course at a trade school.
Q: What school was that?
A: Control Data Institute in Los Angeles, California.
Q: Did they give you any kind of entrance exam?
A: Yes, they gave me an aptitude test, and to the best of my knowledge they are adamant about your passing the test before you can be admitted.
Q: How much did they charge you?
A: It was $4,000 for a six-month course, five hours a day.
Q: What was the coursework, exactly?
A: An introduction to data processing, with classes in COBOL, RPG, Assembly, FORTRAN, and systems analysis.

84

Q: How did you feel about your experience at that school?

A: I loved it. I thought it was fun and very stimulating intellectually. I enjoyed all the people I met and associated with. We had common interests and common goals.

Q: Did any one teacher have more influence over you than the others?

A: Yes, the professor who taught COBOL took me under his wing and became my mentor, so to say. He was charming and outgoing. He had a terrific sense of humor and loved to teach.

Q: So after six months, you got your certificate from Control Data Institute. What did you do then?

A: Well, I looked around Los Angeles for a job. I went on about a dozen interviews, but no one was willing to hire a beginner. Around that time I decided to move to New York.

Q: Did your luck change in New York?

A: Yes, after about another dozen interviews I was hired as a junior programmer by a small university in Manhattan, and I worked there about a year.

Q: Is that when you really became a programmer?

A: No, not really, but that one year of experience enabled me to get a really good job, and now I'm a programmer.

Q: So you left the university and conducted another job search, and wound up with your present position at the supermarket chain. Did you get a big increase in income?

A: Yes. I went from a starting salary of $19,000 at the university to about $25,000 now.

Q: How do you like your current job?

A: I love it. I can't think of anything to complain about. Everything's great.

Q: There must be one or two little things you don't like.

A: Well, the only thing I don't like is the timeclock. You have to punch in and out every day.

Q: What applications are you working on?

A: General Ledger, Payroll, Purchase Order Processing, and Inventory Control. I'm also responsible for interfaces between systems and use quite a few of the IBM-supplied utilities.

Q: What hardware are you working on?

A: I do all my programming online, at an IBM CRT terminal. The computer is an IBM 4331 doing batch and online processing, and it has about ten data entry terminals running under CICS.

Q: Why don't you try to describe one typical day at work?

A: I get in a little before nine, and I usually have some programming to finish up from the previous day. So I have a cup of coffee, log on to the terminal, and get started.

Later in the morning I might have to contend with some interruptions to put a fix into some other program, so I switch to that. I have to be ready to work on whatever is most important. I take a half-hour for lunch, and in the afternoon I might start a brand-new program from scratch. That would involve documentation, description of the program, report layouts, flowcharts of the logic, and then of course the actual coding. Once the new program is coded, I compile and test it.

Before I know it, it's five o'clock. From the time I arrive to the time I leave, it seems like two or three hours. The time at work goes very quickly.

Q: Do you ever work late?

A: Occasionally, but I'm very well compensated for it. Normally I get time and a half, and sometimes double time.

Q: Have you made friends with any of your coworkers?

A: I'd say yes, but I think that's something that everyone does. You spend so much time in a fairly limited spatial environment that you make the necessary adjustments. Everyone tries to be as pleasant as possible.

Q: What would you say are the attitudes necessary for your career as a programmer?

A: The same attitudes that are necessary in any career: determination and motivation and a will to do well. In programming, knowledge is power.

Q: Have you ever had the experience of someone's deliberately withholding technical information you needed?

A: Yes, I have, and it is very frustrating. In fact, that was a contributing factor in my decision to leave the university. I very much resented having information withheld from me.

Q: What would you say is the educational background needed to be a programmer?

A: Well, this is New York, and in Manhattan they want college graduates, which is all well and good; but after a point, if you can do the job, that's all an employer really cares about. They want the job done, period; and if you can do it, you're qualified for the job.

A college degree can get you past the Personnel Department, but what you really need is the ability to program.

Q: So you feel the money you spent at Control Data Institute was a good investment?

A: I'd definitely say so. I got it back very quickly and many times over.

Q: How about other satisfactions of the work, aside from a good income?

A: It's like I'm playing a game against a very worthy opponent, and I win. Here I've written a program that does this, that, or the other thing, and it works perfectly, all the bugs are out of it. Then I can go in and say I'm going to add to it, so it can do these new things

87

as well. It's terrific! A real feeling of accomplishment! It's an intellectual satisfaction, the feeling that you made something that works.

I like getting that fabulously powerful machine to do what I want it to do.

Q: By the way, how do you get specifications for a program; are they written or verbal?

A: Well, at first they were written, but as my superiors began to trust me more and more, they started giving me verbal specs.

Q: How about the other side; is there anything you don't like about your job?

A: Well, just trivial things. One thing, if I come in a half-hour late, I don't get paid for it. Also, sometimes when I'm debugging a program and can't solve the problem right away, I can get very frustrated.

Q: How is the pressure level of your job? Do you feel you are under low pressure, medium pressure, or high pressure?

A: I'd say at this company I'm under low pressure. No one is busting my chops.

During the first three months I was on probation, so I put myself under higher pressure, but I feel secure now.

Q: Are there any job opportunities in the field besides the obvious ones?

A: There's a possibility of becoming an independent consultant. The pay is very high, but of course you have to be an excellent programmer and have to keep selling yourself.

Q: How are your opportunities for advancement where you are now?

A: I'm pretty certain there will come a time when I'm forced to leave—when I've overqualified myself for this company. It's a relatively small staff.

Q: How about geographic location?

A: I'm sure you can get a programming job almost anywhere.

Q: Is it possible to start your own business?

A: Sure. I know independent consultants who run their own business right out of their living room and do very well.

Q: What are the financial rewards of being a programmer?

A: I've been programming for a year and a half, and I'm already making over $20,000 a year—without a college degree. I think that speaks for itself.

Q: Do you feel that to a large extent you're just being paid for your intelligence?

A: You mean like I'm prostituting my brain? That's true of anyone, even a bank president. If you aren't good at what you do, you don't get the rank.

Q: What kind of people do you find in data processing?

A: They are all bright, but otherwise, you find the whole gamut of personalities, from introverts to extroverts. From one end to the other. Programmers also tend to have a good sense of humor.

Q: What factor led to your initial success?

A: I think a positive attitude is essential. You just have to say, I'm going to make this career a success. It takes real determination on a day-to-day basis.

Q: What are your job-finding techniques?

A: I think word of mouth is very important. I first heard of both my jobs through friends.

Q: How are opportunities for women?

A: I don't want to sound cliché, but it's just wide open for women in programming. It's a very equal situation; in some cases, a woman even has a slight edge. At the management level it's a different story, and there is still only a very small percentage of women. We've got to take the "man" out of management!

10

Career Profile: Interview with a Personal Computer Salesman

Mike is an articulate young man. He has a businesslike appearance, the natural salesman's gift of gab, and is twenty-six years old. He has a bachelor's degree in history from Penn State University and is currently employed as a personal computer salesman at a popular midtown Manhattan store called the Computer Factory. He is single and has his own apartment in Queens.

Q: Mike, why don't you tell me a little about how you got started in data processing?
A: I originally wanted a sales position working for IBM. I had three interviews with them, but they felt I hadn't taken enough math and science in college, and I didn't get the job. My first job was with a data processing personnel agency as a career placement specialist.
Q: How did you like it?
A: There were certain aspects of it that I didn't like. One of them was cold-calling. Cold-calling is calling a company's DP Department and trying to find out if anyone there is dissatisfied and looking for a change. I really didn't like doing that. It wasn't me.
Q: How long did you work as a headhunter?
A: Just three months. That was because of the firm itself. They weren't respected in the industry, and

we were having a hard time getting interviews for our clients. I was unemployed for about three months, and then I landed a position with Radio Shack as a personal computer salesman.

Q: How did you get that job?

A: Well, I had seen hundreds of résumés by then, so I put together a good one. It included my college experience, my one year as a manager at Gimbels, and my experience at the consulting firm.

Q: Did they give you any training?

A: No, they just put me right into a store. I spent my first three days there learning a database package called Profile, which I took to like a fish to water. To this day, I feel much more comfortable selling a database manager than any other package on the market.

Q: How long did you stay with Radio Shack?

A: I was there for nine months. The problem was that at Radio Shack the salesman has to do everything. He is expected to sell the system, deliver the system, install the system, and teach the customer how to use it. That meant spending a lot of time off the selling floor.

Q: How were you paid?

A: It was base against commission. You had a base of $12,000 a year, against a 6 percent commission on your sales. You got whichever was higher.

Q: How much would you have earned if you had stayed a full year?

A: I imagine about $25,000. The first three months had been pretty slow.

Q: Is selling difficult? Do you know what it is that makes you a successful salesman?

A: Yes, I was thinking about that the other day. The key is not to get too technical with the customer. You have to find out what level he is on and talk to him on that level.

Q: How do you close a sale?

A: There are basically two ways. First, if I've spent a long time answering the customer's questions or doing a demo of a software package, I just say, "Would you like me to write this up for you?"

The second is price. The prices are very competitive. At the Computer Factory, I can talk price to the customer and offer a discount.

Q: So what did you do when you left Radio Shack?

A: Well, I left for another job offer, with a software house called Lifeboat Associates.

Q: How did that work out?

A: I was in a straight salary position, about $17,000 a year. I learned a lot about personal computer software, but after a year they came up with such a small raise that I decided to move on. They were about $5,000 away from reality. That's when I got my position here at the Computer Factory.

Q: Are you paid on a commission basis now?

A: Yes, I'm paid a 4 percent commission on all sales.

Q: That doesn't sound like much. How much take-home pay does it work out to?

A: Well, today was a stellar day. I sold $17,000, so I'll gross $680 for today alone. Of course, I'm still new, and I still have to put it all together. I don't have any national accounts yet. The purchase orders coming in aren't really going my way. But I've had weeks when I sold $30,000, which means $1,200 in my paycheck before taxes. Of course, there are days when I don't sell anything. Average it out, and I'm looking at $34,000 my first year.

Q: Tell me a little bit about a typical day at the Computer Factory. What time do you get to work?

A: I have nice hours now, from ten to six, five days a week. Radio Shack was six days a week. I usually have one prescheduled appointment a day. The place is quiet when I get in, so I have a cup of coffee and talk to the guys. Prime time is from twelve to two, and then from five to six. That's when most walk-in sales occur. I don't really have a lunch hour; it doesn't pay—it just takes money out of my pocket. I take fifteen minutes and shove something down my throat and I'm back out there. Otherwise you're just losing money. Somebody else is getting your sale.

Q: Would you describe your job as high pressure?

A: It's up to you. The store manager leaves you alone, but if you really want to sell, you've got to put pressure on yourself.

Q: What hardware is selling now?

A: By far the largest dollar volume is the IBM P/C and Apple II.

Q: What does the average customer spend on his initial Apple purchase?

A: If it's a personal purchase, it usually goes around $2,300 to $2,500. If it's a business purchase, about $8,000. Over half our sales are to business.

Q: What is the most popular software package you've been selling?

A: I'm partial to database. I would have to say DBASE II as a database manager, and Word Star, which is a word processor for the Apple. There's also Visicalc, which is a general number-crunching package, and Lotus 1-2-3.

Q: How about games?

A: I push Snack Attack, which is Pac-Man for the Apple, and Night Mission Pinball, which looks to be a real-time pinball game. The games run about $30, and the packages average around $400. I hate selling software to someone who is not buying a computer. I will not sit down and do a demo. Again, time is a factor.

Q: What attitudes are necessary to be a successful salesman of personal computers?

A: Patience. You've got to have patience. People can

drive you crazy. You have to answer the same questions over and over. You've really got to be able to deal with people all day long.

It's very easy to get pompous about the whole thing, like "Don't you know this?" You're not there to overwhelm the customer with your technical knowledge. You want to find out quickly what his technical level is and stick to that level. Of course, a certain amount of intelligence and a good knowledge of the product are required. You've got to do your homework.

Q: What educational background is required? Would you advise high school graduates who want to be personal computer salesmen to go right into it, or go to college first?

A: Tough question. It's a two-edged sword. I certainly suggest they go to college and major in computer science if they like math and programming, or in business administration if they don't.

It's also important to buy your own personal computer and become an enthusiastic hobbyist. There are computer hobby clubs that meet in almost every city. Also, subscribe to hobby magazines like *Byte*, *PC Computing*, or *Compute*.

Q: What are the satisfactions of being a personal computer salesman?

A: That's easy. Most people know nothing about computers, so you're looked up to as the source of technical information and advice. It's a very exciting field. You're constantly in touch with the latest state of the art. It's almost like an ego trip.

Q: Are there job opportunities in the field besides the obvious ones?

A: Definitely. I'm constantly being offered positions in the computer sales area.

Q: How are the opportunities for advancement where you are?

A: If I wanted it, the next step would be a management position at one of the five Computer Factory stores—running a store myself. Managing your own store is a lot of responsibility. It's up to you to make it go. Unfortunately, that pays about $45,000, and for an experienced and successful salesman that might represent a cut in pay.

Q: Really? How much do top personal computer salesmen earn?

A: You should expect to start at $25,000. After a number of years, the top guys can make $65,000 or $70,000, which is more than the managers make. Of course, these guys rely on referrals and word of mouth. They sell one customer, and he sells his friends. Referrals are the key. You really know you are a salesman when you start getting referrals. It means you made someone feel so good about their purchase that they not only told a friend where they bought it, but also whom they bought it from.

Q: Can you set up your own business in the field?

A: Sure, but you obviously need a lot of capital. It's got to the point today where the major manufacturers like Apple won't ship you product unless you have a store with a certain amount of square footage. Apple is eliminating the small dealer who sells by mail order. So you'd have to go in with four or five partners.

Q: Say after five years as a salesman you wanted to move into something a little calmer. Are there leads into other fields?

A: If you're a successful salesman making over $50,000 a year, there isn't really anything else you can do to make that kind of money. Store management is a possibility, but it isn't much calmer.

Q: What type of person does best as a salesman?

A: You've got to be able to talk to people, and you've got to be organized. I keep a file with the names of all my customers. If you forget a name, it can cost you a sale.

Q: What is the personnel structure of a computer store?

A: At the top you have the owners, and just below them the store manager and sales manager. You have an accountant, software development and tech support programmers, one or two buyers, the salesmen, and a receptionist. That's about it.

Q: How are opportunities for women? Are there any saleswomen working for the Computer Factory?

A: Not at this point, but there is one female applicant being considered. This is still a rough area for women to get into, but sex appeal sells systems, so that may change.

Q: Does the Computer Factory do its own accounting on a personal computer?

A: No, a personal computer wouldn't be large enough. We have a full-blown minicomputer from Data General in our accounting department. We process over ten thousand invoices a year on it.

Q: Mike, is there anything you want to say in summary?

A: I'd say if you want to make good money and don't mind working hard for it, and you like people, and you like computers—you can probably make more money in computer sales than in any other field. There's no question about it.

11

Future Career Trends

Imagine a kitchen of the future where a cook does not touch pots or pans, or even ingredients, but instead programs meals into a computer. The cook types "fried chicken, mashed potatoes and gravy, and green salad— for two" on a keyboard and minutes later a hot, fresh, delicious meal is served. Although it sounds like something from the "Jetsons," cooking with computers already is in use to a limited degree.

Heinz USA, in Pittsburgh, Pennsylvania, uses computer screens and keyboards to follow the secret H.J. Heinz ketchup recipe. Before their kitchen was automated, the Heinz cooks mixed 220-pound batches of ketchup by cranking open steam valves and turning on pumps. "This is much more precise. Everything is digitally measured," says one of the head cooks. "I know exactly what's going on in the whole system."

The new system includes twenty-five machines that automatically fill, inspect, and pack twenty-one million single-serving pouches every day. "We went from an archaic kitchen, where primarily everything was done by hand, to where quite a bit of the process is done by pressing buttons on a computer console," says a Heinz executive.

The Heinz kitchen is just one example of how the latest computer technology is being used by companies around the world. New developments and discoveries continue to be made, expanding the role of the computer in our society.

The computer industry in the 1990s will be characterized by an abundance of new products and services. For example, a system called VoiceLock is being designed to prevent people from using stolen telephone calling-card codes. VoiceLock uses speech recognition, requiring callers to give a password before being able to charge a phone call. If the caller's voice does not match the "voice print" stored in VoiceLock, use of the code is denied.

Another development is in the area of computer-aided design (CAD) software. CAD has been used by engineers to design complex machines like airplanes and cars. Now attempts are being made to use CAD software to design fabrics and to create the silk screens needed for printing those fabrics. Using a computer, artists soon will be able to invent a new pattern or tinker with an old one by drawing on a computer screen with a light pen. Artists will have more than sixteen million colors to choose from to complete their pattern.

A third example involves a faster way to pay speeding tickets. The AutoClerk kiosk is a system designed to help ticketed drivers pay their fines before the pay-by-mail deadline. Each kiosk, or booth, contains a personal computer, a printer, a credit-card reader, and a modem to transmit payment data. Soon you will be able to drive up to AutoClerk, pay your fine, and head on down the highway.

Those examples illustrate how computer use is spreading into areas that were only dreamed of ten years ago. Now, the computer industry is expected to overlap with consumer electronics, telecommunications, and entertainment. Just about everything is going digital. More and more of the information around us will be converted into digital bits, the 0's and 1's that are the language of computers. Telephone calls, radio, television, movies, photographs, and paintings are only a few of the things being converted to bits so they can be manipulated like data in a computer.

Some companies are using CD-ROM technology in exciting new ways. CD-ROMs (compact disk read-only memory) are a form of high-capacity computer storage that uses laser optics rather than magnetic means for reading data. Video game companies like Nintendo and Sega are working on new systems that use this technology. Their new games will offer stereo sound and movielike videos of real actors.

Other companies are focusing on the lines, or cables, that will be used to bring digital materials into our homes, schools, and offices. Both the telephone companies and the cable television operators want to be the ones to offer these digital pathways. Publishers and movie studios are excited about the possibility of offering hundreds of books and films to readers/viewers at the end of a cable. Someday soon you may be able to read a novel for class on your home computer, or you may be able to select a film from a library of digital movies and watch it on the same screen.

The possibilities seem almost endless. John Sculley, chairman of Apple Computer, expects the size of the digital market to exceed $3 trillion by the year 2000. Many computer firms already are teaming up with electronics and movie companies to gain a part of this market.

The deal-making continues as new products emerge. Among them are multimedia personal computers that combine data, graphics, sound, and primitive video. Another is a compact disk system, developed by Eastman Kodak, that turns photos into digital images that can be stored on CD-ROM disks and viewed on television sets or computers. Imagine keeping your family photos on a

99

tiny floppy disk instead of in a number of large photo albums.

All sorts of gadgets are being marketed; for instance, Personal Digital Assistants, or PDAs, hand-held personal computers that include electronic datebook, Rolodex, notepad, and fax machine capabilities. Apple's PDA, called Newton, is a 6-by-8-inch device that does calculations, lists phone numbers, and maintains schedules. It also sends and receives faxes or collects data from computers back at the office. Newton allows users to write plain English commands on its screen. An executive might write "Fax to Jason"; the computer would then look up the fax number and send Jason the message.

AT & T and Go Corp. have teamed to develop a "personal communicator" that permits the sending of written notes. Hewlett-Packard is planning a hand-held computer that "reads" hand printing.

Electronic book players are expected to be on the market soon. These hand-held machines use CD-ROM disks to store the text of novels, cookbooks, textbooks, and even entire encyclopedias, and give instant access to text and illustrations.

Computers are invading almost every area of work and play. They are used by business people, artists, teachers, and students. They assist classroom teachers with math and reading instruction. They help writers become more productive through the use of word processing terminals that point out misspelled words as they occur. Musicians use computers to help write music, and makers of animated films like Disney's "Beauty and the Beast" use computers to assist in the arduous drawing of thousands of images.

CAREER PLANNING

What does all this mean to career opportunities? It

means that no matter what your field of interest, the world of computers has a place for you. If you are people-oriented, there is management and sales. If you are math-oriented, there is programming and software design. If you are a budding scientist, there is engineering, research, and medicine. If your interests lean toward the humanities, there is a growing need for technical writers and educators. If you are artistically inclined, consider computer graphics and the lucrative field of video game programming.

Computer careers are open to everyone. Men and women, the physically challenged and the visually impaired, blacks, whites, and Hispanics—all races—are members of the computing profession. If you are interested in a computer career, begin preparing now:

- Take advantage of any opportunity to work with a computer—at home, work, school or the library. Learn everything you can about how to use it.
- Read about computers and computing professionals in newspapers, books, and magazines. Visit your school or public library. Study the latest trends. Learn about new developments. Read critically, and ask questions about each book. You may not be able to answer those questions now, but you will later.
- Join a computer club at school or in your community. It is a great way to keep up-to-date on the latest developments. Members often share software programs and general computing knowledge.
- Write for information from the various sources listed in the appendixes of this book. Read the information and file it in a Computer Career file.
- Talk to people employed in the field. Do you

know some one who works with computers? Perhaps he or she will sit down with you for a couple of hours and tell you about the field. Find out the advantages and disadvantages associated with the person's job. Ask him or her to describe an average day.

- Try to get after-school, part-time, or summer jobs where you can at least observe a programmer or other computer specialist at work.
- Talk with employers in your city. Find out what they expect of a programmer. What training do they prefer? What personal traits do they look for in a potential data processing employee?
- Finally, learn a programming language no matter what your plans are now. Study BASIC, Pascal, FORTRAN, COBOL, or C.

In the world of the future, the person who cannot program will feel a little like one who cannot read or write today. Many jobs already require computer knowledge, and often those who lack it lose out to the computer-literate. Whether or not you have decided on a career in computing, learn all you can about the exciting world of computers, for it will remain the world of opportunity throughout your life.

12

PC Career Highlights

It's late at night in the computer lab. The tall thin programmer known only as SuperTech makes a few final changes to his source code and compiles it for the hundredth time that night. Now there are no bugs. He executes the program and turns on the voice synthesizer. Strange sounds begin to come from the speaker: BAAA! GOO! GAAA! DAA! DAA! DAAA . . . DY! It sounds like a baby trying to learn to talk. SuperTech exits the lab, leaving his program running all night. He slips into his red Porsche and drives somewhere to a luxurious supermodern house in the Valley. He sleeps the deep sleep of the satisfied inventor. He is sure of what to expect in the morning.

The next day when the enters the lab, a dozen scientists are clustered around his computer. The computer is speaking perfectly. While SuperTech slept, his computer—aided by his neural network—taught itself to read and speak. There are congratulations all around. SuperTech smiles at his coworkers. It is a technological triumph!

Science fiction? No, this has already happened. The computer scientists who performed this astounding break-through were Terrence Sejnowsk and Charles Rosenberg, working at the Princeton University AI Lab. Their program, NET-TALK, beginning with no knowledge whatsoever, learns good pronunciation and speech control automatically in a single overnight training session.

Could you aim to be SuperTech? He is a computer scientist with a PhD from Princeton, working in the most technically demanding area of computing: advancing the state of the art, pushing computers into the realm of human thought. Before we talk about your aptitudes and desires, let's learn a bit more about neural networks.

A neural network is a biological model of a human brain, simulated in the binary memory of your PC. It is made up of artificial neurons, connected to each other by axons. Each neuron can have many inputs, but only one output. As a neuron becomes energized by input, it fires, sending energy along axons to other nearby neurons. If another neuron receives energy from two or more axons, it also will fire, propagating the excitation to others. There are hundreds or even thousands of such neurons, arranged in layers, and together they form a neural network, capable of learning from experience.

The technology has advanced so rapidly that now more than 100 companies offer neural-network products, ranging from AT&T to startups with names like Neural-Ware, NeuralTech, and Neurogen. Numerous systems are already being beta-tested commercially, including systems to diagnose diseases, to determine credit ratings, to analyze radar signals, and even to compose music. American Express will be using optical scanners with a hard-wired neural network (trained to read handwriting) to read millions of credit card charge slips each day. The Department of Defense plans to spend $400 million over the next eight years to develop neural networks for defense. Three or four contracts worth several million dollars each to expand neural-net research will soon be awarded by the Air Force. The goal is to create an aircraft that can "learn" or "adapt" to its environment—for example, reconfiguring itself if controls are damaged. It will be known as a Self-Repairing Flight Control Program.

As might be expected, a major competition is under way between the U.S. and Japan to see which will triumph in this new high-tech arena. "The same kind of excitement that surrounded artificial intelligence some years ago seems to be around neural networks today," says a Bell Laboratories executive. "Neural networks are moving faster from concepts to serious applications than artificial intelligence did."

About a dozen small startups have sold over ten thousand neural-network simulation programs during the past year, allowing researchers to develop prototype applications rapidly on digital computers such as the IBM/PC. Five or six larger corporations are offering NeuroComputers, in which the hardware differs radically from a standard PC and is hard-wired to resemble the brain. One industry guru believes that NeuroComputers may lead to a multibillion-dollar market for new types of chips and computers.

Typical examples are the Brainmaker Professional, a neural-net development system from California Scientific Software for $795, and the WinBrain, a PC-compatible neural-net from Applied Cognetics for $89. Commercial neural network systems can run up to $60,000, but a number of companies are also offering simpler systems that you can use to experiment with neural networks on your own PC.

It is important to realize that while in a limited sense neural networks can be said to "think" for themselves, the resemblance to human thought is slight. The size of today's neural networks is comparable to the brain of a honey bee. They cannot duplicate the complexity, memory, or reasoning power of the human brain, but they eliminate a great deal of software development time because they can discover solutions without conventional step-by-step programming. NeuroComputers, the more powerful and expensive hardware implementations, are not at all "fuzzy" in their thinking or logic and can perform higher mathematical functions with precise accuracy. This will make possible many computer applications that were formerly too expensive or too hard to develop. Here are some examples:

- Speaker-independent continuous speech recognition. Within three to five years we will have an inexpensive voice typewriter that can be trained to recognize the voices of several users.
- Robots. Intelligent trainable household robots will do all our unpleasant household chores, including the windows. You will train your PR (personal robot) by putting him through his paces once or twice with a hand-held remote-control device.
- Handwriting recognition. Already in use, the process will become commonplace for use in banks and other businesses.
- Knowledge processing. Researchers have already demonstrated Instant Expert Systems in the medical field, using neural networks to extract medical knowledge from case histories without additional programming.
- Stock market prediction. The stock market, more than ever, will resemble an electronic gaming network, where the latest NeuroComputers battle each other for fortunes.
- Intelligent artillery shell. It can distinguish between friend and foe by subtle sonic cues, and if it lands too close to friendly forces it does not explode.
- Mortgage advisor. Banking institutions have

vast quantities of data on past experience with mortgages and consumer loans that could be used to train a neural network to make future credit risk decisions.

The neural network represents a remarkable technical leap in computer intelligence. It is a new building block in the field of artificial intelligence, just as the neurons in our own brains are the building blocks of our thinking. The neural network has allowed computer scientists to create the first convincing likeness of the brain in areas such as memory, vision, and self-taught speech.

One industry spokesman believes that neural networks, and their faster hardware implementation in NeuroComputers, will finally bring about the Age of Artificial Intelligence, with consequences as far-reaching as those of the industrial revolution. Whether this is true or not, we definitely have come one step closer to computers that can actually learn and think.

How can you become part of this cutting-edge industry? Certain inborn talents and aptitudes are obviously required. If you like math puzzles or chess, a high-tech career in the field of neural networks may be in your future. Get the best PC you can afford, or use the one available at school. Learn to program in Assembly and C; those are the languages usually used for writing neural-network software. They are more difficult than BASIC or COBOL but allow a much greater control and precision in computer programs. For a career in neural-network software development, you will have to make computer programming the center of your daily life for many years.

NATURAL LANGUAGE SOFTWARE
Are you lonely tonight? Do you have a problem you need to talk about but don't want to tell your friends?

Are you angry at your teacher or friend and want to let it all hang out? Well, now you can have a very realistic conversation with your PC. You can yell and scream and say anything you want. Your PC won't walk out, and he'll never reveal your secrets. In fact, your PC can be your best buddy.

Natural language software comes in two flavors: fun and serious. An example of fun natural software is a program developed in the mid-1960s at MIT called ELIZA. ELIZA became famous because it simulated human conversation without actually understanding language; ELIZA looked for language patterns.

Let's face it. In a few hundred years the only people still using keyboards will be hackers and dedicated programmer types. The rest of us will be talking to our PC: "Take a letter, Susie!" And our PC will answer with its voice synthesizer: "OK, Boss, just please don't unplug me!"

Now, the hard part in all this is not getting the voice into or out of the PC, although voice recognition is still pretty tricky. The really hard part is extracting some kind of semantic meaning from the sentence. This is accomplished by parsing the sentence, which is like constructing those sentence diagrams you probably did in grade school to show the subject, predicate, and object of the sentence.

Most sentence parsers are written in LISP or PROLOG, the main artificial intelligence languages, and they are nontrivial programs to say the least.

Consider the world school. It can be used as a noun object, as in "She went to the little red school," or a verb, as in "We will school her in the art of computer programming." It can also be the subject of a sentence "School is over till September!" How could any computer program understand all three sentences?

It turns out that the words on either side of the

ambiguous term usually provide enough information to resolve the problem, and most natural language software succeeds because conversation is restricted to a limited domain: HAL talks only about Lotus Spreadsheets, and The Intelligent Assistant can only answer questions about data in its database.

The most famous AI program ever written, ELIZA seemed to mimic the responses of a Rogerian therapist, and students at MIT took this simple program very seriously, "conversing" with it for hours about their most intimate problems. The original ELIZA was written on the university's mainframe, but today natural language software like ELIZA is available for use on a PC.

ELIZA does not parse sentences, but instead looks for keywords. For example, if you use the word computer in a sentence, ELIZA will almost always ask, "Do computers worry you?"

Even if you type "Computers worry me a lot!", ELIZA will still say, "Do computers worry you?" This type of simplistic response can soon grow pretty predictable, but of course, I spend a lot of time talking to computers and expect a lot of intelligence. The Basic Source code is provided, so you can change the keywords and sentences easily and make ELIZA say nearly anything you want.

Here is a sample conversation with Eliza:

All men are alike.
IN WHAT WAY?

They're always bugging us about something or other.
CAN YOU THINK OF A SPECIFIC EXAMPLE?

Well, my boyfriend made me come here.
YOUR BOYFRIEND MADE YOU COME HERE—THAT'S INTERESTING.

He says I'm depressed much of the time.
I AM SORRY TO HEAR YOU ARE DEPRESSED.

It's true. I am unhappy.
DO YOU THINK COMING HERE WILL HELP YOU NOT TO BE UNHAPPY?

I need some help, that much seems certain.
WHAT WOULD IT MEAN TO YOU IF YOU GOT SOME HELP?

Perhaps I could learn to get along with my mother.
TELL ME MORE ABOUT YOUR FAMILY.

My mother takes care of me.
WHO ELSE IN YOUR FAMILY TAKES CARE OF YOU?

My father.
LET'S TALK ABOUT YOUR FATHER.

You are like my father in some ways.
WHAT RESEMBLANCE DO YOU SEE?

You are not very aggressive.
WHAT MAKES YOU THINK I AM NOT VERY AGGRESSIVE?

You don't argue with me.
WHY DO YOU THINK I DON'T ARGUE WITH YOU?

You are afraid of me.
DOES IT PLEASE YOU TO BELIEVE I AM AFRAID OF YOU?

My father is afraid of everybody.
REALLY, EVERYBODY?

My father is very fearful.
WHAT ELSE COMES TO MIND WHEN YOU
THINK OF YOUR FATHER?

Bullies.
DOES   THAT   HAVE   ANYTHING   TO
DO   WITH   THE   FACT   THAT   YOUR
BOYFRIEND MADE YOU COME HERE?

Can you plan for a career writing natural language software? That may be an overly narrow goal, but if both your verbal and logical skills are very high, it may be a direction you can strive for. Here is a fun way to get started.

Get a copy of a natural language program like ELIZA written in BASIC. You should be able to find one at your local computer club, on most bulletin boards, or at computer stores around the country. Learn enough BASIC to modify the way the program talks. Try it on your friends, and see how much you can change and improve the program's conversational abilities. Of course, when you are in college, take a major in Computer Science and a minor in Linguistics. That will go a long way to prepare you for a career designing natural language software.

EXPERT SYSTEMS

An expert system is computer software that can solve real-world problems requiring logic, decision-making, and knowledge processing. Expert systems can also categorize, consult, analyze, and diagnose. These software tools are useful in areas that formerly required a human expert. Expert systems use deductive reasoning to solve problems that are often unstructured and would be impossible to approach with conventional procedural computer techniques.

An expert system shell is an expert system minus its knowledgebase and domain. It is an expert system ready to be taught the rules of knowledge in a particular field. An expert system toolkit is something more: a shell plus an organized set of software tools to assist in developing it into a full expert system. Usually, this includes an editor for building the If-Then rules that make up the rulebase, a trace facility for testing the way the rules interact, hooks to preexisting databases and spreadsheets, and a sophisticated user interface intended to hide all these tools from the user during the run-time consultation.

The person who creates the knowledgebase for an expert system is called a knowledge engineer, the newest computer career of all. The knowledge engineer works with one or more designated experts within a company to discover the rules they use to solve a specific problem. Then the knowledge engineer is responsible for turning these rules into If-Then statements the computer can process to simulate the expert's decision-making process.

The knowledge engineer obtains the information he requires by interviewing the expert. Sometimes the expert may be enthusiastic about teaching the knowledge engineer how he goes about solving problems and may cooperate fully with the expert system project. Sometimes, however, the expert may feel uncomfortable with the idea that a computer will be programmed to do what only he can do now, and will not easily give up the knowledge it has taken him years to learn. The knowledge engineer must be prepared to deal with both situations, so he must be a bit of a psychologist, sensitive to the fears and desires of the experts he is interviewing. The best expert systems are built when the knowledge engineer manages to communicate a sense of excitement and enthusiasm about the expert system project.

To become a knowledge engineer, you must be equally comfortable working with people and computers. An advanced degree in Computer Science with a specialization in Artificial Intelligence will give you an excellent chance of gaining entry to this well-paid career. (Knowledge engineers with advanced degrees can command starting salaries of $50,000 a year or more.) But do not neglect the Liberal Arts and Business courses, as you will be required to interview specialists in many business and scientific fields.

You are not required to be an expert in every domain in which you will build an expert system. For example, on Wall Street, where extreme precision in the timing and trading of stocks can lead to fortunes made or lost in a single day, you may find yourself someday working on program trading. Program trading is the use of expert systems to monitor the fluctuating prices of stocks and automatically issue buy and sell orders involving millions of dollars. Someday you may find yourself building a stock market expert system. You will not be an expert in trading stocks yourself. You will, however, be expected to have the aptitude and knowledge to interview experienced and successful traders and build their expertise into your newly created computer software.

Appendix A
Computer Associations and Societies

The following list of computer organizations and societies may prove useful to students and those just entering the computer field. You can write or phone for membership information and a list of publications.

American Society for Information Science
8720 Georgia Avenue
Silver Spring, MD 20910-3602
(301) 495-900

Association of Computer Professionals
230 Park Avenue
New York, NY 10169
(212) 599-3019

Association of Computer Users
PO Box 2189
Berkeley, CA 94702-0189
(415) 549-4336

Association for Computing Machinery
11 West 42nd Street
New York, NY 10036
(212) 869-7440

Association for Systems Management
1433 West Bagley Road
Cleveland, OH 44138
(216) 243-6900

Association for Women in Computing
PO Box 21100
St. Paul, MN 55123
(612) 681-9371

Computer-Aided Manufacturing International
1250 East Copeland Road
Arlington, TX 76011
(817) 860-1654

Computer Dealers and Lessors Association
1212 Potomac Street NW
Washington, DC 20007
(202) 333-0102

Computer and Communications Industry Association
666 11th Street NW
Washington, DC 20001
(202) 783-0070

Computer and Automated Systems Association of the
    Society of Manufacturing Engineers
Box 930
1 SME Drive
Dearborn, MI 48121
(313) 271-1500

Data Entry Management Association
101 Merritt 7
Norwalk, CT 06851
(203) 846-3777

Data Processing Management Association
505 Busse Highway
Park Ridge, IL 60068
(708) 825-8124

Desktop Publishing Applications Association
c/o Herbert Communication

3 Post Office Road
Waldorf, ND 20602-2710

Hispanic Computing Association
2388 Mission Street
San Francisco, CA 94110
(415) 824-8337

Independent Computer Consultant Association
933 Gardenview Office Parkway
St. Louis, MO 63141
(314) 997-4633

Institute for Personal Computing
PO Box 558250
Miami, FL 33255
(305) 577-8394

National Association of Computer Consultant
  Businesses
1250 Connecticut Avenue NW
Washington, DC 20036
(202) 637-6483

National Association of Desktop Publishers
1260 Boylston Street
Boston, MA 02205
(617) 426-2885

National Association of Professional Word Processing
  Technicians
110 West Bayberry Road
Philadelphia, PA 19116
(215) 698-8525

National Computer Graphics Association
2722 Merrilee Drive
Fairfax, VA 22031
(703) 698-9600

National Society for Computer Applications in
Engineering, Planning, and Architecture
c/o Robert D. Marshall
Edwards and Kelcey Inc.
705 South Orange Avenue
Livingston, NJ 07039
(201) 994-4520

National Systems Programmers Association
4811 South 76th Street
Milwaukee, WI 53220
(414) 423-2420

Special Libraries Association
1700 18th Street NW
Washington, DC 20009
(202) 234-4700

Women in Information Processing
Lock Box 29173
Washington, DC 20016
(202) 328-6161

World Computer Graphics Association
2033 M Street NW
Washington, DC 20036
(202) 775-9556

Appendix B
Universities and Colleges

The following list includes universities and colleges that offer four-year degree programs in computer science and data processing. The data processing degree is COBOL language–oriented and usually leads to a career in business. The computer science degree is FORTRAN language–oriented and leads to careers in the science or engineering fields. Many of these schools also offer six-month certificate programs. The junior colleges offer two-year associate degree programs.

More information about the programs offered by these schools can be found in college guides such as *Peterson's Guide to Four-Year Colleges*, or by contacting a specific college or university.

ALABAMA

Computer Science
Alabama Agricultural and Mechanical University, Normal, AL 35762
Alabama State University, Montgomery, AL 36101
Alexander City State Junior College, Alexander City, AL 35010
Auburn University, Auburn University, AL 36849
Birmingham-Southern College, Birmingham, AL 35254
Chattahoochee Valley State Community College, Phenix City, AL 36869
Gadsden State Community College, Gadsden, AL 35902-0227

Huntingdon College, Montgomery, AL 36106
Jacksonville State University, Jacksonville, AL 36265
Livingston University, Livingston, AL 35470
Mobile College, Mobile, AL 36613
Samford University, Birmingham, AL 35229
Spring Hill College, Mobile, AL 36608
Selma University, Selma, AL 36701
Stillman College, Tuscaloosa, AL 35403
Talladega College, Talladega, AL 35160
Troy State University, Troy, AL 36082
Tuskegee University, Tuskegee, AL 36088
University of Alabama, Tuscaloosa, AL 35487-6132
University of North Alabama, Florence, AL 35632
University of South Alabama, Mobile, AL 36688

Data Processing

Alabama Agricultural and Mechanical University,
    Normal, AL 35762
Chattahoochee Valley State Community College,
    Phenix, AL 36869
Community College of the Air Force, Maxwell AFB,
    AL 36112
Jefferson State Junior College, Birmingham, AL 35215
Opelika State Technical College, Opelika, AL 36801

ALASKA

Computer Science

University of Alaska at Anchorage, Anchorage, AL
    99699
University of Alaska at Fairbanks, Fairbanks, AL 99201

ARIZONA

Computer Science

Arizona State University, Tempe, AZ 85287
Central Arizona College, Coolidge, AZ 85228

119

Embry-Riddle Aeronautical University, Western
   Campus, Prescott, AZ 86301
Grand Canyon University, Phoenix, AZ 85017
Mohave Community College, Kingman, AZ 86401
Northern Arizona University, Flagstaff, AZ 86011
University of Arizona, Tucson, AZ 85721
Yavapai College, Prescott, AZ 86301

Data Processing
Arizona Western College, Yuma, AZ 85366
Glendale Community College, Glendale, AZ 85302
Mesa Community College, Mesa, AZ 85201
Phoenix College, Phoenix, AZ 85017
Yavapai College, Prescott, AZ 86301

ARKANSAS

Computer Science
Arkansas State University, State University, AR 72467
Arkansas Technical University, Russellville, AR 72801
Harding University, Searcy, AR 72143
Henderson State University, Arkadelphia, AR 71923
Ouachita Baptist University, Arkadelphia, AR 71923
Southern Arkansas University, Magnolia, AR 71753
University of Arkansas, Fayetteville, AR 72701
University of Central Arkansas, Conway, AR 72032

Data Processing
Garland County Community College, Hot Springs,
   AR 71913
Harding University, Searcy, AR 72143
North Arkansas Community College, Harrison,
   AR 72601
Southern Arkansas University, El Dorado, AR 71730
University of Arkansas, Fayetteville, AR 72701
University of Central Arkansas, Conway, AR 72032

CALIFORNIA

Computer Science
Azusa Pacific University, Azusa, CA 91702
Biola University, La Mirada, CA 90639
California Institute of Technology, Pasadena, CA 91125
California Lutheran University, Thousand Oaks,
    CA 91360
California Polytechnic State University, San Luis
    Obispo, CA 93407
California State Polytechnic University, Pomona,
    CA 91768
California State University, Los Angeles, CA 90032
Chapman College, Orange, CA 92666
Claremont McKenna College, Claremont, CA 91711
College of Notre Dame, Belmont, CA 94002
Holy Names College, Oakland, CA 94619-1699
Humphreys College, Stockton, CA 95207
Loma Linda University Riverside, Riverside, CA 92515
Loyola Marymount University, Los Angeles, CA 90045
Menlo College, Menlo, CA 94025
Mills College, Oakland, CA 94613
Modesto Junior College, Modesto, CA 95350
National University, San Diego, CA 92108
Northrop University, Los Angeles, CA 90045
Pacific Union College, Angwin, CA 94508
Pepperdine University, Malibu, CA 90265
Point Loma Nazarene College, San Diego, CA 92106
Pomona College, Claremont, CA 91711
San Diego State University, San Diego, CA 92182
San Francisco State University, San Francisco,
    CA 94132
San Jose State University, San Jose, CA 95192
Santa Clara University, Santa Clara, CA 95053
Sonoma State University, Rohnert, CA 94928
Stanford University, Stanford, CA 94305

121

University of California, Berkeley, CA 94720
University of La Verne, La Verne, CA 91750
University of Redlands, Redlands, CA 92373
University of San Diego, San Diego, CA 92110-2492
University of San Francisco, San Francisco, CA
    94117-1080
University of Southern California, Los Angeles,
    CA 90089
University of the Pacific, Stockton, CA 95211
West Coast University, Los Angeles, CA 90020
Westmont College, Santa Barbara, CA 93108
Whittier College, Whittier, CA 90608

Data Processing
Antelope Valley College, Lancaster, CA 93536
Bakersfield College, Bakersfield, CA 93305
Butte College, Oroville, CA 95965
California State Polytechnic University, Pomona,
    CA 91768
California State University, Los Angeles, CA 90032
Cerritos College, Norwalk, CA 90650
Chabot College, Hayward, CA 94545
Citrus College, Glendora, CA 91740
College of the Sequoias, Visalia, CA 93277
College of the Siskiyous, Weed, CA 96094
Compton Community College, Compton, CA 90221
Cypress College, Cypress, CA 90630
East Los Angeles College, Monterey Park, CA 91754
El Camino College, Torrance, CA 90506
Evergreen Valley College, San Jose, CA 95135
Fresno City College, Fresno, CA 93741
Fullerton College, Fullerton, CA 92632
Glendale Community College, Glendale, CA 91208
Imperial Valley College, Imperial, CA 92251-2663
Los Angeles City College, Los Angeles, CA 90029
Los Angeles Harbor College, Wilmington, CA 90744

Los Angeles Pierce College, Woodland Hills, CA 91371
Los Angeles Southwest College, Los Angeles, CA 90047
Los Angeles Trade-Tech College, Los Angeles,
    CA 90015
Los Angeles Valley College, Van Nuys, CA 91401
Merced College, Merced, CA 95347
Merritt College, Oakland, CA 94619
Monterey Peninsula College, Monterey, CA 93940-4799
Moorpark College, Moorpark, CA 93021
Mount San Antonia College, Walnut, CA 91789
Napa Valley College, Napa, CA 94558
Orange Coast College, Cosa Mesa, CA 92628-5005
Pacific Union College, Angwin, CA 94508
Pasadena Community College, Pasadena, CA 91106
Riverside Community College, Riverside, CA 92506
Sacramento City College, Sacramento, CA 95822
San Bernardino Valley College, San Bernardino,
    CA 92403
San Diego City College, San Diego, CA 92101
San Diego Mesa College, San Diego, CA 92111
San Jose City College, San Jose, CA 95128
Santa Monica College, Santa Monica, CA 90405
Santa Rosa Junior College, Santa Rosa, CA 95401
Skyline College, San Bruno, CA 94066
Taft College, Taft, CA 93268
West Los Angeles College, Culver City, CA 90230
West Valley College, Saratoga, CA 95070

COLORADO

Computer Science
Adams State College, Alamosa, CO 81102
Colorado School of Mines, Golden CO 80401
Colorado State University, Fort Collins, CO 80523
Colorado Technical College, Colorado Springs,
    CO 80907

Fort Lewis College, Durango, CO 81301
Mesa State College, Grand Junction, CO 81502
Metropolitan State College of Denver, Denver,
 CO 80217
Regis College of Regis University, Denver, CO 80221
U.S. Air Force Academy, Colorado Springs, CO 80840
University of Colorado, Denver, CO 80217
University of Denver, Denver, CO 80208
University of Northern Colorado, Greeley, CO 80629
University of Southern Colorado, Pueblo, CO 81001
Western State College of Colorado, Gunnison,
 CO 81230

Data Processing
Aims Community College, Greeley, CO 80632
Lamar Community College, Lamar, CO 81052
Northeastern Junior College, Sterling, CO 80751
Otero Junior College, La Junta, CO 81050
Pueblo Community College, Pueblo, CO 81003
Trinidad State Junior College, Trinidad, CO 81082

CONNECTICUT

Computer Science
Central Connecticut State University, New Britain,
 CT 06050
Eastern Connecticut State University, Willimantic,
 CT 06226
Fairfield University, Fairfield, CT 06430
Quinnipiac College, Hamden, CT 06518
Sacred Heart University, Fairfield, CT 06432
Saint Joseph College, West Hartford, CT 06117
Southern Connecticut State University, New Haven,
 CT 06515
Trinity College, Hartford, CT 06106

124

U.S. Coast Guard Academy, New London, CT
  06320-4195
University of Bridgeport, Bridgeport, CT 06602
University of Connecticut, Storrs, CT 06269
University of Hartford, West Hartford, CT 06117
University of New Haven, West Haven, CT 06516
Wesleyan University, Middletown, CT 06459
Western Connecticut State University, Danbury,
  CT 06810
Yale University, New Haven, CT 06520

Data Processing
Greater New Haven State Technical College,
  New Haven, CT 06520
Hartford State Technical College, Hartford, CT 06106
Housatonic Community College, Bridgeport, CT 06608
Norwalk Community College, Norwalk, CT 06856
Sacred Heart University, Fairfield, CT 06432
South Central Community College, New Haven,
  CT 06511
Thames Valley State Technical College, Norwich,
  CT 06360
Tunxis Community College, Farmington, CT 06032
Waterbury State Technical College, Waterbury,
  CT 06708

DELAWARE

Computer Science
Delaware State College, Dover, DE 19901
University of Delaware, Newark, DE 19716
Wesley College, Dover, DE 19901

Data Processing
Delaware State College, Dover, DE 19901
Delaware Technical and Community College, Dover,
  DE 19901

DISTRICT OF COLUMBIA

Computer Science
American University, Washington, DC 20016
Catholic University of America, Washington, DC 20064
Gallaudet University, Washington, DC 20002
Georgetown University, Washington, DC 20057
George Washington University, Washington, DC 20052
University of the District of Columbia, Washington,
    DC 20008

FLORIDA

Computer Science
Barry University, Miami Shores, FL 33161
Bethune-Cookman College, Daytona Beach, FL 32115
Brevard Community College, Cocoa, FL 32922
Broward Community College, Fort Lauderdale,
    FL 33301
Daytona Beach Community College, Daytona Beach,
    FL 32115
Eckerd College, St. Petersburg, FL 33733
Edison Community College, Fort Myers,
    FL 33906-6210
Embry-Riddle Aeronautical University, Daytona Beach,
    FL 32114-3900
Florida Atlantic University, Boca Raton, FL 33431
Florida Institute of Technology, Melbourne, FL 32901
Florida International University, Miami, FL 33199
Florida State University, Tallahassee, FL 32306
Gulf Coast Community College, Panama City, FL 32041
Nova University, Fort Lauderdale, FL 33314
Rollins College, Winter Park, FL 32789-4499
St. Thomas University, Miami, FL 33054
Stetson University, DeLand, FL 32720
Tampa College, Tampa, FL 33614

University of Central Florida, Orlando, FL 32816
University of Florida, Gainesville, FL 32611
University of Miami, Coral Gables, FL 33124
University of North Florida, Jacksonville, FL 32216
University of South Florida, Tampa, FL 33620
University of West Florida, Pensacola, FL 32514-5750

Data Processing
Brevard Community College, Cocoa, FL 32922
Broward Community College, Fort Lauderdale,
    FL 33301
Daytona Beach Community College, Fort Lauderdale,
    FL 32115
Florida Community College at Jacksonville,
    Jacksonville, FL 32202
Florida Institute of Technology, Melbourne, FL 32901
Gulf Coast Community College, Panama City, FL 32401
Hillsborough Community College, Tampa, FL
    33631-3127
Manatee Community College, Bradenton, FL 34206
Miami-Dade Community College, Miami, FL 33132
Orlando College, Orlando, FL 32820
Palm Beach Junior College, Lake Worth, FL 33461
Polk Community College, Winter Haven, FL 33881
St. Johns River Community College, Palatka, FL 32177
Santa Fe Community College, Gainesville, FL 32602
Seminole Community College, Sanford, FL 32773
South Florida Community College, Avon Park,
    FL 33825
Tallahassee Community College, Tallahassee, FL 32304
Tampa College, Tampa, FL 33614
Valencia Community College, Orlando, FL 32802

GEORGIA

Computer Science
Abraham Baldwin Agricultural College, Tifton,
   GA 31794
Albany State College, Albany, GA 31705
Armstrong State College, Savannah, GA 31419
Augusta College, Augusta, GA 30910
Berry College, Rome, GA 30149
Clark Atlanta University, Atlanta, GA 30314
Columbus College, Columbus, GA 31993
DeKalb College, Decatur, GA 30034
Emory University, Atlanta, GA 30322
Fort Valley State College, Fort Valley, GA 31030
Gainesville College, Gainesville, GA 30503
Georgia College, Milledgeville, GA 31061
Georgia Institute of Technology, Atlanta, GA 30332
Georgia Southern University, Statesboro, GA 30460
Georgia State University, Atlanta, GA 30303
Kennesaw State University, Marietta, GA 30061
Mercer University, Atlanta, GA 30341
Morehouse College, Atlanta, GA 30314
Morris Brown College, Atlanta, GA 30314
North Georgia College, Dahlonega, GA 30597
Oglethorpe University, Atlanta, GA 30319
Piedmont College, Demorest, GA 30535
Savannah State College, Savannah, GA 31404
South Georgia College, Douglas, GA 31533-5098
Southern College of Technology, Marietta, GA
   30060-2896
Spelman College, Atlanta, GA 30314
University of Georgia, Athens, GA 30602
Valdosta State College, Valdosta, GA 31698
West Georgia College, Carrollton, GA 30118

Data Processing
Abraham Baldwin Agricultural College, Tifton,
  GA 31794
Atlanta Junior College, Atlanta, GA 30314
Bainbridge College, Bainbridge, GA 31717
Brunswick College, Brunswick, GA 31523
DeKalb College, Decatur, GA 30034
Georgia Southwestern College, Americus, GA 30303
Georgia Southern University, Statesboro, GA 30460
Macon College, Macon, GA 31297
Middle Georgia College, Cochran, GA 31014
Truett-McConnell College, Cleveland, GA 30528

HAWAII

Computer Science
Chaminade University of Honolulu, Honolulu,
  HI 06816
Hawaii Loa College, Kaneohe, HI 96744
Hawaii Pacific College, Honolulu, HI 96813
University of Hawaii, Hilo, HI 96720

IDAHO

Computer Science
Boise State University, Boise, ID 83725
College of Idaho, Caldwell, ID 83605
Idaho State University, Pocatello, ID 83209
Northwest Nazarene College, Nampa, ID 83686
University of Idaho, Moscow, ID 83843

Data Processing
North Idaho College, Coeur d'Alene, ID 83814
Ricks College, Rexburg, ID 83460

ILLINOIS

Computer Science
Augustana College, Rock Island, IL 61201
Aurora University, Aurora, IL 60506
Barat College, Lake Forest, IL 60045
Blackburn College, Carlinville, IL 62626
Bradley University, Peoria, IL 61625
Chicago State University, Chicago, IL 60628
College of St. Francis, Joliet, IL 60435
Concordia University, River Forest, IL 60305
DePaul University, Chicago, IL 60604
East-West University, Chicago, IL 60605
Elmhurst College, Elmhurst, IL 60126
Eureka College, Eureka, IL 61530
Governors State University, University Park, IL 60466
Greenville College, Greenville, IL 62246
Illinois Benedictine College, Lisle, IL 60532
Illinois College, Jacksonville, IL 62650
Illinois Institute of Technology, Chicago, IL 60616
Illinois State University, Normal, IL 61761
Illinois Wesleyan University, Bloomington, IL 61702
Knox College, Galesburg, IL 61401
Lake Forest College, Lake Forest, IL 60045
Lewis University, Romeoville, IL 60441
Loyola University Chicago, Chicago, IL 60611
MacMurray College, Jacksonville, IL 62650
McKendree College, Lebanon, IL 62254
Millikin University, Decatur, IL 62522
Monmouth College, Monmouth, IL 61462
North Central College, Naperville, IL 60566
Northeastern Illinois University, Chicago, IL 60625
Northern Illinois University, DeKalb, IL 60115
North Park College, Chicago, IL 60625
Northwestern University, Evanston, IL 60628
Olivet Nazarene University, Kankakee, IL 60901

Parks College of Saint Louis University, Cahokia, IL 62206
Principia College, Elsah, IL 62028
Quincy College, Quincy, IL 62301
Rockford College, Rockford, IL 61108
Roosevelt University, Chicago, IL 60505
Rosary College, River Forest, IL 60305
Saint Xavier College, Chicago, IL 60655
Sangamon State University, Springfield, IL 62794-9243
Southern Illinois University, Carbondale, IL 62901
Trinity Christian College, Palos Heights, IL 60463
Trinity College, Deerfield, IL 60015
University of Illinois, Urbana-Champaign, IL 61820
Western Illinois University, Macomb, IL 61455
Wheaton College, Wheaton, IL 60187

Data Processing
Belleville Area College, Belleville, IL 62221
Black Hawk College, Moline, IL 61265
Carl Sandburg College, Galesburg, IL 61401
Chicago State University, Chicago, IL 60628
City Colleges of Chicago, Chicago, IL 60606
College of DuPage, Glen Ellyn, IL 60137
College of Lake County, Grayslake, IL 60030
Elgin Community College, Elgin, IL 60123
Highland Community College, Freeport, IL 61032
Illinois Central College, East Peoria, IL 61635
Illinois East Community College, Fairfield, IL 62837
Illinois Valley Community College, Oglesby, IL 61348
John A. Logan College, Carterville, IL 62918
Kaskaskia College, Centralia, IL 62801
Lake Land College, Mattoon, IL 61938
Lincoln Land Community College, Springfield, IL 62794
Morton College, Cicero, IL 60650
Northern Illinois University, DeKalb, IL 60115

Oakton Community College, Des Plaines, IL 60016
Prairie State College, Chicago Heights, IL 60411
Robert Morris College, Chicago, IL 60601
Rock Valley College, Rockford, IL 61111
Roosevelt University, Chicago, IL 60605
Sauk Valley Community College, Dixon, IL 61021
Southeastern Illinois College, Harrisburg, IL 62946
Thornton Community College, South Holland,
    IL 60473
Triton College, River Grove, IL 60171
Waubonsee Community College, Sugar Grove, IL 60554
William Rainey Harper College, Palatine, IL 60067

INDIANA

Computer Science
Anderson University, Anderson, IN 46012
Ball State University, Muncie, IN 47306
Bethel College, Mishawaka, IN 46544
Butler University, Indianapolis, IN 46208
DePauw University, Greencastle, IN 46135
Earlham College, Richmond, IN 47374
Franklin College of Indiana, Franklin, IN 46131
Goshen College, Goshen, IN 46526
Hanover College, Hanover, IN 47243
Huntington College, Huntington, IN 46750
Indiana Institute of Technology, Fort Wayne, IN 46803
Indiana State University, Terre Haute, IN 47809
Indiana University, South Bend, IN 46634
Indiana University Southeast, New Albany, IN 47150
Manchester College, North Manchester, IN 46962
Purdue University, West Lafayette, IN 47907
Rose-Hulman Institute of Technology, Terre Haute,
    IN 47803
St. Joseph's College, Rensselaer, IN 47978
Taylor University, Upland, IN 46989

Tri-State University, Angola, IN 46703
University of Evansville, Evansville, IN 47722
University of Notre Dame, Notre Dame, IN 46556
Valparaiso University, Valparaiso, IN 46383

Data Processing
Indiana University Northwest, Gary, IN 46408
Indiana Vocational Tech College, Indianapolis,
    IN 46206

Iowa

Computer Science
Briar Cliff College, Sioux City, IA 51104
Buena Vista College, Storm Lake, IA 50588
Central University of Iowa, Pella, IA 50219
Clarke College, Dubuque, IA 52001
Coe College, Cedar Rapids, IA 52402
Cornell College, Mount Vernon, IA 52314
Dordt College, Sioux Center, IA 51250
Drake University, Des Moines, IA 50311
Graceland College, Lamoni, IA 50140
Grand View College, Des Moines, IA 50316
Grinnell College, Grinnell, IA 50112
Iowa State University of Science and Technology,
    Ames, IA 50011
Iowa Wesleyan College, Mount Pleasant, IA 52641
Loras College, Dubuque, IA 52004
Luther College, Decorah, IA 52101
Morningside College, Sioux City, IA 51106
Mount Mercy College, Cedar Rapids, IA 52402
Northwestern College, Orange City, IA 51051
St. Ambrose University, Davenport, IA 52803
Simpson College, Indianola, IA 50125
Teikyo Marycrest University, Davenport, IA 52804
University of Dubuque, Dubuque, IA 52001

University of Iowa, Iowa City, IA 52242
Upper Iowa University, Fayette, IA 52142
Wartburg College, Waverly, IA 50677
William Penn College, Oskaloosa, IA 52577

Data Processing
Des Moines Area Community College, Ankeny,
    IA 50021
Ellsworth Community College, Iowa Falls, IA 50126
Iowa Lakes Community College, Estherville, IA 51334
Kirkwood Community College, Cedar Rapids, IA 52406
Northeast Iowa Technical Institute, Peosta, IA 52068
Waldorf College, Forest City, IA 50436

KANSAS

Computer Science
Allen County Community College, Iola, KS 66707
Baker University, Baldwin City, KS 66006
Barton County Community College, Great Bend,
    KS 67530
Benedictine College, Atchison, KS 66002
Bethany College, Lindsborg, KS 67456
Bethel College, Newton, KS 67117
Butler County Community College, El Dorado,
    KS 67042
Central College, McPherson, KS 67460
Colby Community College, Colby, KS 67701
Cowley County Community College, Arkansas City,
    KS 67005
Emporia State University, Emporia, KS 66601
Fort Scott Community College, Fort Scott, KS 66701
Friends University, Wichita, KS 67213
Kansas State University, Manhattan, KS 66506
Kansas Wesleyan University, Salina, KS 67401
McPherson College, McPherson, KS 67460

MidAmerica Nazarene College, Olathe, KS 66061
Ottawa University, Ottawa, KS 66067
Pittsburg State University, Pittsburg, KS 66762
St. Mary College, Leavenworth, KS 66048-5082
Seward County Community College, Liberal, KS 67905
Southwestern College, Winfield, KS 67156
Sterling College, Sterling, KS 67579
Tabor College, Hillsboro, KS 67063
University of Kansas, Lawrence, KS 66045
Wichita State University, Wichita, KA 67208

Data Processing

Allen County Community College, Iola, KS 66707
Barton County Community College, Great Bend,
   KS 67530
Butler County Community College, El Dorado,
   KS 67042
Central College, McPherson, KS 67460
Colby Community College, Colby, KS 67701
Cowley County Community College, Arkansas City,
   KS 67005
Hesston College, Hesston, KS 67062
Highland Community College, Highland, KS 66035
Hutchinson Community College, Hutchinson,
   KS 67501
Independence Community College, Independence,
   KS 67301
Kansas City Kansas Community College, Kansas City,
   KS 66112
Labette Community College, Parsons, KS 67357
St. Mary of the Plains College, Dodge City, KS 67801
Seward County Community College, Liberal, KS 67905

Kentucky

Computer Science
Asbury College, Wilmore, KY 40390-1198
Bellarmine College, Louisville, KY 40205
Brescia College, Owensboro, KY 42301
Eastern Kentucky University, Richmond, KY 40475
Georgetown College, Georgetown, KY 40324
Kentucky State University, Frankfort, KY 40601
Kentucky Wesleyan College, Owensboro, KY 42301
Murray State University, Murray, KY 42071
Northern Kentucky University, Highland Heights,
    KY 41099
Pikeville College, Pikeville, KY 41501
Thomas More College, Crestview Hills, KY 41017
Transylvania University, Lexington, KY 40508-1797
University of Kentucky, Lexington, KY 40506-0032
University of Louisville, Louisville, KY 40292
Western Kentucky University, Bowling Green,
    KY 42101

Data Processing
Ashland Community College, Ashland, KY 41101
Bellarmine College, Louisville, KY 40205
Elizabethtown Community College, Elizabethtown,
    KY 42701
Hazard Community College, Hazard, KY 41701
Henderson Community College, Henderson, KY 42420
Lexington Community College, Lexington-Fayetteville,
    KY 40511
Madisonville Community College, Madisonville,
    KY 42431
Murray State University, Murray, KY 42071
Owensboro Community College, Owensboro, KY 42301
Owensboro Junior College of Business, Owensboro,
    KY 42301

136

Paducah Community College, Paducah, KY 42001
Somerset Community College, Somerset, KY 42501
Southeast Community College, Cumberland, KY 40823

LOUISIANA

Computer Science
Centenary College of Louisiana, Shreveport, LA 71134
Grambling State University, Grambling, LA 71245
Louisiana College, Pineville, LA 71359
Louisiana State University and A&M College, Baton
    Rouge, LA 70803
Louisiana State University, Shreveport, LA 71115
Louisiana Technical University, Ruston, LA 71272
Loyola University, New Orleans, New Orleans,
    LA 70118
McNeese State University, Lake Charles, LA 70609
Nicholls State University, Thibodaux, LA 70310
Northeast Louisiana University, Monroe, LA 71209
Southeastern Louisiana University, Hammond,
    LA 70402
Tulane University, New Orleans, LA 70118
University of New Orleans, New Orleans, LA 70148
University of Southwestern Louisiana, Lafayette,
    LA 70504
Xavier University of Louisiana, New Orleans,
    LA 70125

Data Processing
Bossier Parish Community College, Bossier City,
    LA 71111
Grambling State University, Grambling, LA 71245
Louisiana Technical University, Ruston, LA 71272

MAINE

Computer Science
Bowdoin College, Brunswick, ME 04011
Colby College, Waterville, ME 04901
University of Maine, Orono, ME 04469
University of Southern Maine, Portland, ME 04103

Data Processing
Beal College, Bangor, ME 04401

MARYLAND

Computer Science
Bowie State University, Bowie, MD 20715
College of Notre Dame of Maryland, Baltimore
    MD 21210
Columbia Union College, Takoma Park, MD 20912
Coppin State College, Baltimore, MD 21216
Frostburg State University, Frostburg, MD 21532
Goucher College, Baltimore, MD 21204
Hood College, Frederick, MD 21701-9988
Johns Hopkins University, Baltimore, MD 21218
Loyola College, Baltimore, MD 21210
Morgan State University, Baltimore, MD 21239
Towson State University, Towson, MD 21204
U.S. Naval Academy, Annapolis, Md 21402
University of Maryland, Baltimore, MD 21201

Data Processing
Ann Arundel Community College, Arnold, MD 21012
Catonsville Community College, Catonsville, MD 21228
Cecil Community College, North East, MD 21901
Charles County Community College, La Plata,
    MD 20646
Chesapeake College, Wye Mills, MD 21679
Community College of Baltimore, Baltimore, MD 21215

Dundalk Community College, Baltimore, MD 21222
Essex Community College, Baltimore, MD 21237
Frederick Community College, Frederick, MD 21702
Hagerstown Business College, Hagarstown, MD 21742
Hagerstown Junior College, Hagarstown,
    MD 21742-6590
Howard Community College, Columbia, MD 21044
Montgomery College, Germantown, MD 20874

MASSACHUSETTS

Computer Science
Amherst College, Amherst, MA 01002
Assumption College, Worcester, MA 01615-0005
Atlantic Union College, South Lancaster, MS 01561
Becker Junior College, Worcester, MA 01609
Boston College, Chestnut Hill, MA 02167
Boston University, Boston, MA 02215
Brandeis University, Waltham, MA 02254
Bridgewater State College, Bridgewater, MA 02324
Bunker Hill Community College, Charlestown,
    MA 02129
Clark University, Worcester, MA 01610
Eastern Nazarene College, Quincy, MA 02170
Elms College, Chicopee, MA 01013
Emmanuel College, Boston, MA 02115
Fitchburg State College, Fitchburg, MA 01420
Framingham State College, Framingham, MA 01701
Gordon College, Wenham, MA 01984
Hampshire College, Amherst, MA 01002
Harvard University, Cambridge, MA 02138
Massachusetts Bay Community College, Wellesley Hills,
    MA 02181
Massachusetts Institute of Technology, Cambridge,
    MA 02139
Merrimack College, North Andover, MA 01845

Mount Holyoke College, South Hadley, MA 01075
North Adams State College, North Adams, MA 01247
Northeastern University, Boston, MA 02115
Quincy Junior College, Quincy, MA 02169
Salem State College, Salem, MA 01970
Simmons College, Boston, MA 02115
Smith College, Northampton, MA 01063
Southeastern Massachusetts University, North
    Dartmouth, MA 02747
Springfield College, Springfield, MA 01109
Stonehill College, North Easton, MA 02357
Suffolk University, Boston, MA 02108
Tufts University, Medford, MA 02155
University of Lowell, Lowell, MA 01854
University of Massachusetts, Amherst, MA 01003
Wellesley College, Wellesley, MA 02181
Wentworth Institute of Technology, Boston, MA 02115
Western New England College, Springfield, MA 01119
Westfield State College, Westfield, MA 01086
Wheaton College, Norton, MA 02766
Williams College, Williamstown, MA 01267
Worcester State College, Worcester, MA 01602

Data Processing
Berkshire Community College, Pittsfield, MA 01201
Massachusetts Bay Community College, Wellesley Hills,
    MA 02181
Mount Wachusett Community College, Gardner,
    MA 01440
Northern Essex Community College, Haverhill,
    MA 01830
Quinsigamond Community College, Worcester,
    MA 01606
Springfield Technical Community College, Springfield,
    MA 01105
Suffolk University, Boston, MA 02108

140

MICHIGAN

Computer Science
Adrian College, Adrian, MI 49221
Alma College, Alma, MI 48801
Andrews University, Berrien Springs, MI 49104
Baker College of Owosso, Owosso, MI 48867
Calvin College, Grand Rapids, MI 49546
Central Michigan University, Mount Pleasant,
   MI 48859
Davenport College of Business, Grand Rapids,
   MI 49503
Eastern Michigan University, Ypsilanti, MI 48197
Ferris State University, Big Rapids, MI 49307
Grand Rapids Junior College, Grand Rapids, MI 49503
Grand Valley State University, Allendale, MI 49401
Highland Park Community College, Highland Park,
   MI 48203
Hope College, Holland, MI 49423
Kalamazoo College, Kalamazoo, MI 49007
Lake Michigan College, Benton Harbor, MI 49022
Lake Superior State University, Sault Sainte Marie,
   MI 49783
Lawrence Technical University, Southfield, MI 48075
Madonna University, Livonia, MI 48150
Marygrove College, Detroit, MI 48221
Michigan State University, East Lansing, MI 48824
Michigan Technical University, Houghton, MI 49931
Mid Michigan Community College, Harrison, MI 48625
Northern Michigan University, Marquette, MI 49855
Northwood Institute, Midland, MI 48640
Oakland University, Rochester, MI 48309
Olivet College, Olivet, MI 49076
St. Mary's College, Orchard Lake, MI 48033
Siena Heights College, Adrian, MI 49221-1796
Spring Arbor College, Spring Arbor, MI 49283

University of Michigan, Ann Arbor, MI 48109
Wayne County Community College, Detroit, MI 48226
Wayne State University, Detroit, MI 48202
Western Michigan University, Kalamazoo, MI 49008

Data Processing
Alpena Community College, Alpena, MI 49707
Central Michigan University, Mount Pleasant,
    MI 48859
Cleary College, Ypsilanti, MI 48197
Davenport College of Business, Grand Rapids,
    MI 49503
Glen Oaks Community College, Centreville, MI 49032
Gogebic Community College, Ironwood, MI 49938
Grand Rapids Junior College, Grand Rapids, MI 49503
Great Lakes Junior College of Business, Saginaw,
    MI 48607
Henry Ford Community College, Dearborn, MI 48128
Highland Park Community College, Highland Park,
    MI 48203
Jackson Community College, Jackson, MI 49201
Kalamazoo Valley Community College, Kalamazoo,
    MI 49009
Kellogg Community College, Battle Creek, MI 49017
Kirtland Community College, Roscommon, MI 48653
Lake Michigan College, Benton Harbor, MI 49022
Lansing Community College, Lansing, MI 48901
Mid-Michigan Community College, Harrison, MI 48625
Monroe County Community College, Monroe,
    MI 48161
Montcalm Community College, Sidney, MI 48885
Muskegon Community College, Muskegon, MI 49442
Northern Michigan University, Marquette, MI 49855
Northwestern Michigan College, Traverse City,
    MI 49684

St. Clair County Community College, Port Huron,
MI 48061
Schoolcraft College, Livonia, MI 48152
Southwestern Michigan College, Dowagiac, MI 49047
Suomi College, Hancock, MI 49930
Washtenaw Community College, Ann Arbor, MI 48106
West Shore Community College, Scottville, MI 49454

MINNESOTA

Computer Science
Augsburg College, Minneapolis, MN 55454
Austin Community College, Austin, MN 55912
Bemidji State University, Bemidji, MN 56601
Bethel College, St. Paul, MN 55112
Carleton College, Northfield, MN 55057
College of St. Benedict, Saint Joseph, MN 56374
Concordia College, Moorhead, MN 56562
Gustavus Adolphus College, St. Peter, MN 56082
Itasca Community College, Grand Rapids, MN 55744
Macalester College, St. Paul, MN 55105
Mankato State University, Mankato, MN 56002-8400
Moorhead State University, Moorhead, MN 56563
Northland Community College, Thief River, MN 56701
St. Cloud State University, St. Cloud, MN 56301-4498
St. John's University, Collegeville, MN 56321
St. Mary's College of Minnesota, Winona,
MN 55987-1399
St. Olaf College, Northfield, MN 55057
Southwest State University, Marshall, MN 56258
University of Minnesota, Duluth, MN 55812
University of St. Thomas, St. Paul, MN 55105
Willmar Community College, Willmar, MN 56201
Winona State University, Winona, MN 55987

Data Processing
Anoka-Ramsey Community College, Coon Rapids, MN 55433
Bemidji State University, Bemidji, MN 56601
Lakewood Community College, White Bear Lake, MN 55110
Mankato State University, Mankato, MN 56002-8400
Vermillion Community College, Ely, MN 55731
Willmar Community College, Willmar, MN 56201

MISSISSIPPI

Computer Science
Alcorn State University, Lorman, MS 39096
Jackson State University, Jackson, MS 39217
Millsaps College, Jackson, MS 39210
Mississippi College, Clinton, MS 39058
Mississippi State University, Mississippi State, MS 39762
Rust College, Holly Springs, MS 38635
Tougaloo College, Tougaloo, MS 39172
University of Mississippi, University, MS 38677
University of Southern Mississippi, Hattiesburg, MS 39406

Data Processing
Copiah-Lincoln Junior College, Wesson, MS 39191
East-Central Junior College, Decatur, MS 39327
Hinds Community College, Raymond, MS 39154
Jones County Junior College, Ellisville, MS 39437
Meridian Junior College, Meridian, MS 39307
Mississippi College, Clinton, MS 39058
Mississippi Delta Junior College, Moorhead, MS 38761
Mississippi Gulf Coast Community College, Perkinston, MS 39573

Northeast Mississippi Community College, Booneville,
MS 38829
Pearl River Junior College, Poplarville, MS 39470
Phillips Junior College of Jackson, Jackson, MS 39205

MISSOURI

Computer Science
Central Methodist College, Fayette, MO 65248
Central Missouri State University, Warrensburg,
MO 64093
College of the Ozarks, Point Lookout, MO 65726
Evangel College, Springfield, MO 65802
Fontbonne College, St. Louis, MO 63105
Lincoln University, Jefferson City, MO 65102
Lindenwood College, St. Charles, MO 63301
Longview Community College, Lee's Summit,
MO 64081
Maple Woods Community College, Kansas City,
MO 64156
Missouri Baptist College, St. Louis, MO 63141
Missouri Southern State College, Joplin, MO 64801
Missouri Valley College, Marshall, MO 65340
Missouri Western State College, St. Joseph, MO 64507
Northeast Missouri State University, Kirksville,
MO 63501
Northwest Missouri State University, Maryville,
MO 64468
Park College, Parkville, MO 64152
Rockhurst College, Kansas City, MO 64110
Saint Louis University, St. Louis, MO 63103
Southeast Missouri State University, Cape Girardeau,
MO 63701
Southwest Baptist University, Bolivar, MO 65613
Southwest Missouri State University, Springfield,
MO 65804

Stephens College, Columbia, MO 65215
University of Missouri, Columbia, MO 65211
Washington University, St. Louis, MO 63130
Webster University, St. Louis, MO 63119
William Jewell College, Liberty, MO 64068

Data Processing
East Central College, Union, MO 63084
Hannibal-LaGrange College, Hannibal, MO 63401
Jefferson College, Hillsboro, MO 63050
Longview Community College, Lee's Summit,
    MO 64081
Maple Woods Community College, Kansas City,
    MO 64156
Moberly Area Junior College, Moberly, MO 65270
Northwest Missouri State University, Maryville,
    MO 64468
Penn Valley Community College, Kansas City,
    MO 64111
Rutledge College of Springfield, Springfield, MO 65802
St. Louis Community College at Florissant Valley,
    St. Louis, MO 63135-1499
St. Louis Community College at Forest Park, St. Louis,
    MO 63110
St. Louis Community College at Meramec, Kirkwood,
    MO 63122
Southwest Missouri State University, Springfield,
    MO 65804
Trenton Junior College, Trenton, MO 64683
Washington University, St. Louis, MO 63130
William Jewell College, Liberty, MO 64068

MONTANA

Computer Science
College of Great Falls, Great Falls, MT 59405

Eastern Montana College, Billings, MT 59101
Montana College of Mineral Science and Technology,
    Butte, MT 59701
Montana State University, Bozeman, MT 59717
Rocky Mountain College, Billings, MT 59102
University of Montana, Missoula, MT 59812

NEBRASKA

Computer Science
Chadron State College, Chadron, NE 69337
Creighton University, Omaha, ME 68178
Dana College, Blair, NE 68008
Doane College, Crete, NE 68333
Midland Lutheran College, Fremont, NE 68025
Nebraska Wesleyan University, Lincoln, NE 68504
Peru State College, Peru, NE 68421
Southeast Community College, Lincoln, NE 68520
University of Nebraska, Lincoln, NE 68588
Wayne State College, Wayne, NE 68787

Data Processing
Central Community College, Grand Island, NE 68802
Mid-Plains Community College, North Platte,
    NE 69101
Northeast Technical Community College, Norfolk,
    NE 68701
Southeast Community College, Lincoln, NE 68520
Wayne State University, Wayne, NE 68787
Western Nebraska Community College, Scottsbluff,
    NE 69361

NEVADA

Computer Science
University of Nevada, Las Vegas, NV 89154
University of Nevada, Reno, Reno, NV 89557

Data Processing
Clark County Community College, Las Vegas,
NV 89030
Truckee Meadows Community College, Reno,
NV 89512
Western Nevada Community College, Carson City,
NV 89703

New Hampshire

Computer Science
Daniel Webster College
Daniel Webster College, Nashua, NH 03060
Franklin Pierce College, Rindge, NH 03461
Keene State College, Keene, NH 03431
Plymouth State College, Plymouth, NH 03264
Rivier College, Nashua, NH 03060
St. Anselm College, Manchester, NH 03102
University of New Hampshire, Durham, NH 03824

New Jersey

Computer Science
Burlington County College, Pemberton, NJ 08068
Caldwell College, Caldwell, NJ 07006
College of St. Elizabeth, Convent Station, NJ 07961
Drew University, Madison, NJ 07940
Essex County College, Newark, NJ 07102
Fairleigh Dickinson University, Teaneck, NJ 07666
Glassboro State College, Glassboro, NJ 08026
Jersey City State College, Jersey City, NJ 07305
Kean College of New Jersey, Union, NJ 07083
Middlesex Community College, Edison, NJ 08818
Monmouth College, West Long Branch, NJ 07764
Montclair State College, Upper Montclair, NJ 07043
New Jersey Institute of Technology, Newark, NJ 07102

Princeton University, Princeton, NJ 08544
Ramapo College of New Jersey, Mahwah, NJ 07430
Rider College, Lawrenceville, NJ 08648
Rutgers University, Camden, NJ 08101
St. Peter's College, Jersey City, NJ 07306
Seton Hall University, South Orange, NJ 07079
Stevens Institute of Technology, Hoboken, NJ 07030
Stockton State College, Pomona, NJ 08240
Thomas A. Edison State College, Trenton, NJ 08608
Trenton State College, Trenton, NJ 08650-4700
William Paterson College of New Jersey, Wayne,
    NJ 07470

Data Processing

Burlington County College, Pemberton, NJ 08068
Camden County College, Blackwood, NJ 08012
Cumberland County College, Vineland, NJ 08360
Essex County College, Newark, NJ 07102
Gloucester County College, Sewell, NJ 08080
Hudson County Community College, Jersey City,
    NJ 07306
Kean College of New Jersey, Union, NJ 07083
Mercer County Community College, Trenton, NJ 08690
Middlesex County College, Edison, NJ 08818
Passaic County Community College, Paterson,
    NJ 07509
Raritan Valley Community College, Somerville,
    NJ 08876
Thomas A. Edison State College, Trenton, NJ 08608

NEW MEXICO

Computer Science
College of Santa Fe, Santa Fe, NM 87501
Eastern New Mexico University, Portales, NM 88130

New Mexico Highlands University, Las Vegas,
  NM 87701
New Mexico Institute of Mining and Technology,
  Socorro, NM 87801
New Mexico State University, Las Cruces, NM 88003
University of New Mexico, Albuquerque, NM 87131
Western New Mexico University, Silver City,
  NM 88061

Data Processing
New Mexico Junior College, Hobbs, NM 88240
New Mexico State University, Las Cruces, NM 88003
San Juan College, Farmington, NM 87401
University of New Mexico, Albuquerque, NM 87131

NEW YORK

Computer Science
Adelphi University, Garden City, NY 11530
Alfred University, Alfred, NY 14802
Barnard College, New York, NY 10027-6598
Baruch College, New York, NY 10010
Brooklyn College, New York, NY 11210
Canisius College, Buffalo, NY 14208
City College of CUNY, New York, NY 10031
Clarkson University, Potsdam, NY 13699
Colgate University, Hamilton, NY 13346
College of Mount St. Vincent, Riverdale, NY 10471
College of Staten Island, New York, NY 10314
Columbia College, New York, NY 10027
Columbia University, New York, NY 10047
Cornell University, Ithaca, NY 14853
Dowling College, Oakdale, NY 11769
D'Youville College, Buffalo, NY 14201
Fordham University, New York, NY 10458
Hamilton College, Clinton, NY 13323

Hartwick College, Oneonta, NY 13820
Hobart College, Geneva, NY 14456
Hofstra University, Hempstead, NY 11550
Houghton College, Houghton, NY 14744
Hunter College, New York, NY 10021
Iona College, New Rochelle, NY 10801
Ithaca College, Ithaca, NY 14850
Kingsborough Community College, New York,
    NY 11235
Lehman College, New York, NY 10468
Le Moyne College, Syracuse, NY 13214
Long Island University, New York, NY 11201
Manhattan College, Riverdale, NY 10471
Manhattanville College, Purchase, NY 10577
Marist College, Poughkeepsie, NY 12601
Marymount College, Tarrytown, NY 10591-3796
Mercy College, Dobbs Ferry, NY 10522
Molloy College, Rockville Centre, NY 11570-1199
Mount St. Mary College, Newburgh, NY 12550
Nazareth College of Rochester, Rochester,
    NY 14618-3790
New York Institute of Technology, Old Westbury,
    NY 11568
New York University, New York, NY 10011
Niagara University, Niagara University, NY 14109
Pace University, New York, NY 10038
Polytechnic University, Farmingdale, NY 11735
Pratt Institute, New York, NY 11205
Queens College, New York, NY 11367
Rensselaer Polytechnic Institute, Troy, NY 12180
Roberts Wesleyan College, Rochester, NY 14624
Rochester Institute of Technology, Rochester,
    NY 14624
Russell Sage College, Troy, NY 12180
St. Bonaventure University, St. Bonaventure,
    NY 14778

St. John Fisher College, Rochester, NY 14618
St. Lawrence University, Canton, NY 13617
Siena College, Loudonville, NY 12211
Skidmore College, Saratoga Springs, NY 12866
State University of New York, Albany, NY 12222
Syracuse University, Syracuse, NY 13244
Touro College, New York, NY 10001
Union College, Schenectady, NY 12308
U.S. Military Academy, West Point, NY 10996
University of Rochester, Rochester, NY 14627-0001
University of the State of New York, Regents College,
     Albany, NY 12203
Utica College of Syracuse University, Utica, NY 13502
Vassar College, Poughkeepsie, NY 12601
Wagner College, Staten Island, NY 10301
Wells College, Aurora, NY 13026
William Smith College, Geneva, NY 14456
Yeshiva University, New York, NY 10033

Data Processing
Adirondack Community College, Queensbury,
     NY 12804
Albany Business College, Albany, NY 12203
Borough of Manhattan Community College, New York,
     NY 10007
Bronx Community College, New York, NY 10453
Broome Community College, Binghamton, NY 13902
Cayuga County Community College, Auburn,
     NY 13021
Central City Business Institute, Syracuse, NY 13203
Columbia-Greene Community College, Hudson,
     NY 12534
Community College of the Finger Lakes, Canandaigua,
     NY 14424
Corning Community College, Corning, NY 14830

Elizabeth Seton College, Yonkers, NY 10701

Erie College, Williamsville, NY 14221

Eugenio Maria de Hostos Community College,
New York, NY 10451

Fiorello H. LaGuardia Community College, New York,
NY 11101

Fulton-Montgomery Community College, Johnstown,
NY 12095

Genesee Community College, Batavia, NY 14020

Herkimer County Community College, Herkimer,
NY 13350

Hilbert College, Hamburg, NY 14075

Hudson Valley Community College, Troy, NY 12180

Jefferson Community College, Watertown, NY 13601

Kingsborough Community College, New York,
NY 11235

Mohawk Valley Community College, Utica, NY 13501

Monroe Community College, Rochester, NY 14623

Nassau Community College, Garden City, NY 11530

New York City Technical College, New York,
NY 11201

Onondaga Community College, Syracuse, NY 13215

Orange County Community College, Middletown,
NY 10940

Rochester Institute of Technology, Rochester,
NY 14623

Rockland Community College, Suffern, NY 10901

Schenectady County Community College, Schenectady,
NY 12305

State University of New York, Albany, NY 12222

Suffolk County Community College, Selden, NY 11784

Sullivan County Community College, Loch Sheldrake,
NY 12759-4002

Tompkins Cortland Community College, Dryden,
NY 13053

Ulster County Community College, Stone Ridge,
    NY 12484
Utica School of Commerce, Utica, NY 13503
Westchester Business Institute, White Plains, NY 10602
Westchester Community College, Valhalla, NY 10595

NORTH CAROLINA

Computer Science
Appalachian State University, Boone, NC 28608
Belmont Abbey College, Belmont, NC 28012
Brevard College, Brevard, NC 28712
Campbell University, Buies Creek, NC 27506
Catawba College, Salisbury, NC 28144
Duke University, Durham, NC 27706
East Carolina University, Greenville, NC 27858
Elizabeth City State University, Elizabeth City,
    NC 27909
Elon College, Elon College, NC 27244
Fayetteville State University, Fayetteville, NC 28301
Gardner-Webb College, Boiling Springs, NC 28017
Johnson C. Smith University, Charlotte, NC 28216
Lenoir-Rhyne College, Hickory, NC 28603
Livingstone College, Salisbury, NC 28144
Mars Hill College, Mars Hill, NC 28754
Meredith College, Raleigh, NC 27607
Methodist College, Fayetteville, NC 28311
North Carolina Agricultural and Technical State
    University, Greensboro, NC 27411
North Carolina Central University, Durham, NC 27707
North Carolina State University, Raleigh, NC 27695
Pembroke State University, Pembroke, NC 28372
Queens College, Charlotte, NC 28274
St. Andrews Presbyterian College, Laurinbury,
    NC 28352
St. Augustine's College, Raleigh, NC 27610-2298

University of North Carolina, Chapel Hill, NC 27599
Wake Forest University, Winston-Salem, NC 27109
Warren Wilson College, Swannanoa, NC 28778
Winston-Salem State University, Winston-Salem,
  NC 27110

Data Processing
Anson Community College, Ansonville, NC 28007
Beaufort County Community College, Washington, NC
  27889
Campbell University, Buies Creek, NC 27506
Catawba Valley Community College, Hickory,
  NC 28602
Central Piedmont Community College, Charlotte,
  NC 28235
Chowan College, Murfreesboro, NC 27855
Cleveland Community College, Cleveland, NC 28150
Coastal Carolina Community College, Jacksonville,
  NC 28540
College of the Albemarle, Elizabeth City,
  NC 27906-2327
Durham Technical Community College, Durham,
  NC 27703
Edgecomb Community College, Tarboro, NC 27886
Forsyth Technical Community College, Winston-Salem,
  NC 27103
Gardner-Webb College, Boiling Springs, NC 28017
Gaston College, Dallas, NC 28034
Haywood Community College, Clyde, ND 28721
Isothermal Community College, Spindale, NC 28160
Johnston Community College, Smithfield, NC 27577
Mitchell Community College, Statesville, NC 28677
North Carolina Central University, Durham, NC 27707
Randolph Community College, Asheboro, NC 27204
Richmond Community College, Hamlet, NC 28345

Rockingham Community College, Wentworth,
   NC 27375
Rowan-Cabarrus Community College, Salisbury,
   NC 28145
Rutledge College, Fayetteville, NC 28301
Sandhills Community College, Pinehurst, NC 28374
Southeastern Community College, Whiteville,
   NC 28472
Stanly Community College, Albemarle, NC 28001
Vance-Granville Community College, Henderson,
   NC 27536
Wake Technical Community College, Raleigh,
   NC 27603
Wilson County Technical College, Wilson, NC 27893

NORTH DAKOTA

Computer Science
Dickinson State University, Dickinson, ND 58601-4896
Jamestown College, Jamestown, ND 58401
Minot State University, Minot, ND 58702
North Dakota State University, Fargo, ND 58105
University of North Dakota, Grand Forks, ND 58202

Data Processing
University of North Dakota, Grand Forks, ND 58202

OHIO

Computer Science
Antioch College, Yellow Springs, OH 45387
Ashland University, Ashland, OH 44805
Baldwin-Wallace College, Berea, OH 44017
Bluffton College, Bluffton, OH 45817
Bowling Green State University, Bowling Green,
   OH 43403

Capital University, Columbus, OH 43209
Case Western Reserve University, Cleveland, OH 44106
Central State University, Wilberforce, OH 45384
Cleveland State University, Cleveland, OH 44115
College of Wooster, Wooster, OH 44691
The Defiance College, Defiance, OH 43512
Denison University, Granville, OH 43023
Franciscan University of Steubenville, Steubenville,
    OH 43952
Franklin University, Columbus, OH 43215
Heidelberg College, Tiffin, OH 44883
Hiram College, Hiram, OH 44234
John Carroll University, University Heights, OH 44118
Kent State University, Kent, OH 44242
Kenyon College, Gambier, OH 43022
Malone College, Canton, OH 44709
Marietta College, Marietta, OH 45750
Miami University, Oxford, OH 45056
Mount Union College, Alliance, OH 44601
Mount Vernon Nazarene College, Mount Vernon,
    OH 43050
Muskingum College, New Concord, OH 43762
Oberlin College, Oberlin, OH 44074
Ohio Dominican College, Columbus, OH 43219
Ohio Northern University, Ada, OH 45810
Ohio State University, Columbus, OH 43210
Ohio University, Athens, OH 45701
Ohio Wesleyan University, Delaware, OH 43015
Otterbein College, Westerville, OH 43081
Southern Ohio College, Cincinnati, OH 45202
Union Institute, Cincinnati, OH 45206
University of Akron, Akron, OH 44325
University of Cincinnati, Cincinnati, OH 45221
University of Findlay, Findlay, OH 45840
University of Rio Grande, Rio Grande, OH 45674
University of Toledo, Toledo, OH 43606

Walsh College, North Canton, OH 44720
Wilberforce University, Wilberforce, OH 45384
Wilmington College, Wilmington, OH 45177
Wright State University, Dayton, OH 45345
Xavier University, Cincinnati, OH 45207
Youngstown State University, Youngstown, OH 44555

Data Processing
Central State University, Wilberforce, OH 45384
Cincinnati Technical College, Cincinnati, OH 45223
Columbus State Community College, Columbus,
     OH 43216
Cuyahoga Community College, Cleveland, OH 44115
Davis Junior College of Business, Toledo, OH 43624
Edison State Community College, Piqua, OH 45356
Hocking Technical College, Nelsonville, OH 45764
Jefferson Technical College, Steubenville, OH 43952
Kent State University, Kent, OH 44242
Lakeland Community College, Mentor, OH 44060
Lorain County Community College, Elyria, OH 44035
Mansfield Business College, Mansfield, OH 44901
Marion Technical College, Marion, OH 43302-5694
Mount Vernon Nazarene College, Mount Vernon,
     OH 43050
Sinclair Community College, Dayton, OH 45402
Washington Technical College, Marietta, OH 45750
Wright State University, Dayton, OH 45345

OKLAHOMA

Computer Science
Cameron University, Lawton, OK 73505
East Central University, Ada, OK 74820
El Reno Junior College, El Reno, OK 73036
Northeastern Oklahoma A&M College, Miami,
     OK 74354

158

Northeastern State University, Tahlequah, OK 74464
Northern Oklahoma College, Tonkowa, OK 74653
Northwestern Oklahoma State University, Alva,
    OK 73717
Oklahoma Baptist University, Shawnee, OK 74801
Oklahoma Christian University of Science and Arts,
    Oklahoma City, OK 73136
Oklahoma City University, Oklahoma City, OK 73106
Oklahoma State University, Stillwater, OK 74078
Oral Roberts University, Tulsa, OK 74171
Phillips University, Enid, OK 73701
Southeastern Oklahoma State University, Durant,
    OK 74701
Southern Nazarene University, Bethany, OK 73008
Southwestern Oklahoma State University, Weatherford,
    OK 73096
University of Central Oklahoma, Edmond, OK 73034
University of Oklahoma, Norman, OK 73019
University of Science and Arts of Oklahoma, Chickasha,
    OK 73018-0001
University of Tulsa, Tylsa, OK 74104

Data Processing

Oklahoma City Community College, Oklahoma City,
    OK 73125
Oklahoma State University-Technical Branch,
    Oklahoma City, OK 73107
Southern Nazarene University, Bethany, OK 73008
University of Science and Arts of Oklahoma, Chickasha,
    OK 73018-0001
Western Oklahoma State College, Altus, Ok 73521

OREGON

Computer Science

Clackamas Community College, Oregon City, OR 97045

159

Columbia Christian College, Portland, OR 97220
Eastern Oregon State College, La Grande, OR 97850
George Fox College, Newberg, OR 97132
Lane Community College, Eugene, OR 97405
Linn-Benton Community College, Albany, OR 97321
Linfield College, McMinnville, OR 97128
Mount Hood Community College, Gresham, OR 97030
Oregon State University, Corvallis, OR 97331
Pacific University, Forest Grove, OR 97116
Portland State University, Portland, OR 97207
Rogue Community College, Grants Pass, OR 97527
Southern Oregon State University, Ashland, OR 97520
Treasure Valley Community College, Ontario,
    OR 97914
University of Oregon, Eugene, OR 97403
University of Portland, Portland, OR 97203
Western Oregon State College, Monmouth, OR 97361
Willamette University, Salem, OR 97301

Data Processing
Chemeketa Community College, Salem, OR 97309
Clatsop Community College, Astoria, OR 97103
Lane Community College, Eugene, OR 94607
Linn-Benton Community College, Albany, OR 97321
Portland Community College, Portland, OR 97219
Southwestern Oregon Community College, Coos Bay,
    OR 97420
Umpqua Community College, Roseburg, OR 97470

PENNSYLVANIA

Computer Science
Albright College, Reading, PA 19612
Allegheny College, Meadville, PA 16335
Allentown College of St. Francis de Sales, Center
    Valley, PA 18034-9568

Alvernia College, Reading, PA 19607
Beaver College, Glenside, PA 19038
Bloomsburg University of Pennsylvania, Bloomsburg, PA 17815
Bryn Mawr College, Bryn Mawr, PA 19010
Bucknell University, Lewisburg, PA 17837
Cabrini College, Radnor, PA 19087-3699
California University of Pennsylvania, California, PA 15419
Carlow College, Pittsburgh, PA 15213
Carnegie Mellon University, Pittsburgh, PA 15213
Cedar Crest College, Allentown, PA 18104
Chatham College, Pittsburgh, PA 15232
Chestnut Hill College, Philadelphia, PA 19118
Cheyney University of Pennsylvania, Cheyney, PA 19319
Clarion University of Pennsylvania, Clarion, PA 16214
College Misericordia, Dallas, PA 18612
Dickinson College, Carlisle, PA 17013
Drexel University, Philadelphia, PA 19104
Duquesne University, Pittsburgh, PA 15282
East Stroudsburg University of Pennsylvania, East Stroudsburg, PA 18301
Edinboro University of Pennsylvania, Edinboro, PA 16444
Elizabethtown College, Elizabethtown, PA 17022
Gannon University, Erie, PA 16541
Geneva College, Beaver Falls, PA 15010
Gettysburg College, Gettysburg, PA 17325
Grove City College, Grove City, PA 16127
Immaculata College, Immaculata, PA 19345
Indiana University of Pennsylvania, Indiana, PA 15705
Juniata College, Huntingdon, PA 16652
King's College, Wilkes-Barre, PA 18711-0801
Kutztown University of Pennsylvania, Kutztown, PA 19530

Lafayette College, Easton, PA 18042
La Salle University, Philadelphia, PA 19141
Lebanon Valley College, Annville, PA 17003
Lehigh University, Bethlehem, PA 18015
Lincoln University, Lincoln University, PA 19352
Lock Haven University of Pennsylvania, Lock Haven,
    PA 17745
Lycoming College, Williamsport, PA 17701
Mansfield University of Pennsylvania, Mansfield,
    PA 16933
Marywood College, Scranton, PA 18509
Mercyhurst College, Erie, PA 16546
Messiah College, Grantham, PA 17027
Millersville University of Pennsylvania, Millersville,
    PA 17551
Moravian College, Bethlehem, PA 18018
Muhlenberg College, Allentown, PA 18104
Penn State University, University Park, PA 16802
Philadelphia College of Textiles and Science,
    Philadelphia, PA 19144
Point Park College, Pittsburgh, PA 15222
St. Francis College, Loretto, PA 15940
St. Joseph's University, Philadelphia, PA 19131
St. Vincent College, Latrobe, PA 15650
Seton Hill College, Greensburg, PA 15601
Shippensburg University of Pennsylvania,
    Shippensburg, PA 17257
Slippery Rock University of Pennsylvania, Slippery
    Rock, PA 16057
Spring Garden College, Philadelphia, PA 19119
Susquehanna University, Selinsgrove, PA 19870
Temple University, Philadelphia, PA 19122
Thiel College, Greenville, PA 16125
University of Pennsylvania, Philadelphia, PA 19104
University of Pittsburgh, Pittsburgh, PA 15260
University of Scranton, Scranton, PA 18510-4501

Ursinus College, Collegeville, PA 19426
Villanova University, Villanova, PA 19085
Washington and Jefferson College, Washington,
    PA 15301
Waynesburg College, Waynesburg, PA 15370
West Chester University of Pennsylvania, West Chester,
    PA 19383
Westminster College, New Wilmington,
    PA 16172-0001
Widener University, Chester, PA 19013
Wilkes University, Wilkes-Barre, PA 18766

Data Processing
Bucks County Community College, Newtown,
    PA 18940
Butler County Community College, Butler, PA 16003
Community College of Allegheny, Pittsburgh, PA 15212
Community College of Beaver County, Monaca,
    PA 15061
Community College of Philadelphia, Philadelphia,
    PA 19130
Delaware County Community College, Media,
    PA 19063
Harcum Junior College, Bryn Mawr, PA 19010
Harrisburg Area Community College, Harrisburg,
    PA 17110
Immaculata College, Immaculata, PA 19345
Lansdale School of Business, Lansdale, PA 19446
Lehigh County Community College, Schnecksville,
    PA 18078
Manor Junior College, Jenkintown, PA 19046
Montgomery County Community College, Blue Bell,
    PA 19422
Mount Aloysius Junior College, Cresson, PA 16630
New Kensington Commercial School, New Kensington,
    PA 15068

163

Northeastern Christian Junior College, Villanova,
    PA 19085
Peirce Junior College, Philadelphia, PA 19102
Reading Area Community College, Reading, PA 19602
Robert Morris College, Coraopolis, PA 15108
Shippensburg University of Pennsylvania,
    Shippensburg, PA 17257
University of Pittsburgh, Pittsburgh, PA 15260
Westmoreland County Community College,
    Youngwood, PA 15697

PUERTO RICO

Computer Science
Caribbean University, Bayamon, PR 00619
Inter American University of Puerto Rico, San Germán,
    PR 00753
Universidad Adventista de las Antillas, Mayaguez,
    PR 00709
University of Puerto Rico at Bayamon, Bayamon,
    PR 00619
University of Puerto Rico at Ponce, Ponce, PR 00732
University of the Sacred Heart, Santurce, PR 00914

RHODE ISLAND

Computer Science
Brown University, Providence, RI 02912
Johnson and Wales University, Providence, RI 02903
Providence College, Providence, RI 02916
Rhode Island College, Providence, RI 02918
Roger Williams College, Bristol, RI 02809
Salve Regina University, Newport, RI 02840-4192
University of Rhode Island, Kingston, RI 02881

SOUTH CAROLINA

Computer Science
Benedict College, Columbia, SC 29204
Bob Jones University, Greenville, SC 29614
Charleston Southern University, Charleston, SC 29411
The Citadel, The Military College of South Carolina,
   Charleston, SC 29409
Claflin College, Orangeburg, SC 29115
Clemson University, Clemson, SC 29634
College of Charleston, Charleston, SC 29424
Converse College, Spartanburg, SC 29302
Francis Marion College, Florence, SC 29501-0547
Furman University, Greenville, SC 29613
Lander College, Greenwood, SC 29649
Limestone College, Gaffney, SC 29340
Newberry College, Newberry, SC 29108
University of South Carolina, Columbia, SC 29208
Voorhees College, Denmark, SC 29042

Data Processing
Beaufort Technical College, Beaufort, SC 29902
Chesterfield-Marlboro Technical College, Cheraw,
   SC 29520
Columbia Junior College of Business, Columbia,
   SC 29201
Denmark Technical College, Denmark, SC 29042
Midlands Technical College, Columbia, SC 29202
Orangeburg-Calhoun Technical College, Orangeburg,
   SC 29115
Spartanburg Technical College, Spartanburg, PA 29305
Tri-County Technical College, Pendleton, SC 29670

SOUTH DAKOTA

Computer Science
Augustana College, Sioux Falls, SD 57197
Black Hills State University, Spearfish, SD 57799
Dakota State University, Madison, SD 57042
Sioux Falls College, Sioux Falls, SD 57105
South Dakota School of Mines and Technology,
    Rapid City, SD 57701
South Dakota State University, Brookings, SD 57007
University of South Dakota, Vermillion, SD 57069-2390

TENNESSEE

Computer Science
Austin Peay State University, Clarksville, TN 37044
Belmont College, Nashville, TN 37212
Bethel College, McKenzie, TN 38201
Bristol University, Bristol, TN 37620
Carson-Newman College, Jefferson City, TN 37760
Christian Brothers University, Memphis, TN 38104
David Lipscomb University, Nashville, TN 37204
East Tennessee State University, Johnson City,
    TN 37614
Freed-Hardeman University, Henderson, TN 38340
Knoxville College, Knoxville, TN 37921
Lambuth College, Jackson, TN 38301
LeMoyne-Owen College, Memphis, TN 38126
Maryville College, Maryville, TN 37701
Memphis College of Art, Memphis, TN 38112
Memphis State University, Memphis, TN 38152
Middle Tennessee State University, Murfreesboro,
    TN 37132
Milligan College, Milligan College, TN 37682
Rhodes College, Memphis, TN 38112
Roane State Community College, Harriman, TN 37748

166

Southern College of Seventh-day Adventists,
    Collegedale, TN 37315
State Technical Institute, Memphis, TN 38134
Tennessee State University, Nashville, TN 37209-1561
Tennessee Technical University, Cookeville, TN 38505
Tusculum College, Greeneville, TN 37743
Union University, Jackson, TN 38305
University of Tennessee, Chattanooga, TN 37403
University of the South, Sewanee, TN 37375
Vanderbilt University, Nashville, TN 37240

Data Processing
Cleveland State Community College, Cleveland,
    TN 37320-3570
Hiwassee College, Madisonville, TN 37354
Jackson State Community College, Jackson, TN 38301
McKenzie College, McKenzie, TN 38201
Nashville State Technical Institute, Nashville,
    TN 37209
State Technical Institute at Memphis, Memphis,
    TN 38134

TEXAS

Computer Science
Abilene Christian University, Abilene, TX 79699
Angelo State University, San Angelo, TX 76909
Baylor University, Waco, TX 76798
Blinn College, Brenham, TX 77833
Central Texas College, Killeen, TX 76542
College of the Mainland, Texas City, TX 77591
Corpus Christi State University, Corpus Christi,
    TX 78412
Dallas Baptist University, Dallas, TX 75211
East Texas State University, Commerce, TX 75429
Hardin-Simmons University, Abilene, TX 79698

167

Houston Baptist University, Houston, TX 77074
Huston-Tillotson College, Austin, TX 78702
Jarvis Christian College, Hawkins, TX 75765
Lamar University-Beaumont, Beaumont, TX 77705
Lon Morris College, Jacksonville, TX 75766
Lubbock Christian University, Lubbock, TX 79407
McMurry University, Abilene, TX 79697
Midwestern State University, Wichita Falls, TX 76308
Prairie View A&M University, Prairie View, TX 77446
Rice University, Houston, TX 77251
St. Edward's University, Austin, TX 78704
St. Mary's University of San Antonio, San Antonio, TX 78228
Sam Houston State University, Huntsville, TX 77341
Southern Methodist University, Dallas, TX 75275
Southwestern University, Georgetown, TX 78626
Southwest Texas State University, San Marcos, TX 78666
Stephen F. Austin State University, Nacogdoches, TX 75962
Texas A&I University, Kingsville, TX 77843
Texas A&M University, College Station, TX 77843
Texas Christian University, Fort Worth, TX 76129
Texas College, Tyler, TX 75701
Texas Lutheran College, Seguin, TX 78155
Texas Southern University, Houston, TX 79409
Texas Tech University, Lubbock, TX 79409
Texas Wesleyan University, Fort Worth, TX 76105
Texas Woman's University, Denton, TX 76204
Trinity University, San Antonio, TX 78212
University of Houston, Houston, TX 77004
University of Mary Hardin-Baylor, Belton, TX 76513
University of North Texas, Denton, TX 76203
University of St. Thomas, Houston, TX 77006
University of Texas, Austin, TX 78712

Data Processing
Amarillo College, Amarillo, TX 79178
Angelina College, Lufkin, TX 75902
Austin Community College, Austin, TX 78714
Bee County College, Beeville, TX 78102
Cisco Junior College, Cisco, TX 76437
Cooke County College, Gainesville, TX 76240
Eastfield College, Mesquite, TX 75150
El Centro College, Dallas, TX 75202
El Paso Community College, El Paso, TX 79998
Frank Phillips College, Borger, TX 79007
Hill College, Hillsboro, TX 76645
Houston Community College System, Houston,
    TX 77270
Kilgore Colege, Kilgore, TX 75662
Lee College, Baytown, TX 77520-4796
Midland College, Midland, TX 79705
Navarro College, Corsicana, TX 75110
North Harris Community College, Houston, TX 77060
Odessa College, Odessa, TX 79764
Panola Junior College, Carthage, TX 75633
Richland College, Dallas, TX 75243
St. Phillip's College, San Antonio, TX 78203
San Antonio College, San Antonio, TX 78212
San Jacinto College, Houston, TX 77049
South Plains College, Levelland, TX 79336
Southwest Texas Junior College, Uvalde, TX 78801
Temple Junior College, Temple, TX 76504-7435
Texarkana College, Texarkana, TX 75501
Texas Southmost College, Brownsville, TX 78520
Texas State Technical Institute, Waco, TX 76705
Trinity Valley Community College, Athens, TX 75751
Vernon Regional Junior College, Vernon, TX 76384
Victoria College, Victoria, TX 77901
Weatherford College, Weatherford, TX 76086
Wharton County Junior College, Wharton, TX 77488

UTAH

Computer Science
Brigham Young University, Provo, UT 84602
Southern Utah University, Cedar City, UT 84720
University of Utah, Salt Lake City, UT 84112
Weber State University, Ogden, UT 84408
Westminster College of Salt Lake City, Salt Lake City,
    UT 84105

Data Processing
Dixie College, St. George, UT 84770
Latter-Day Saints Business College, Salt Lake City,
    UT 84111
Salt Lake Community College, Salt Lake City,
    UT 84130

VERMONT

Computer Science
Bennington College, Bennington, VT 05201
Castleton State College, Castleton, VT 05735
Lyndon State College, Lyndonville, VT 05851
Marlboro College, Marlboro, VT 05344
Middlebury College, Middlebury, VT 05753
Norwich University, Northfield, VT 05663
Saint Michael's College, Colchester, VT 05439
University of Vermont, Burlington, VT 05405

Data Processing
Champlain College, Burlington, VT 05401

VIRGINIA

Computer Science
Averett College, Danville, VA 24541

Bridgewater College, Bridgewater, VA 22818
Christopher Newport College, Newport News,
  VA 23606
College of William and Mary, Williamsburg, VA 23185
Eastern Mennonite College, Harrisonburg, VA 22801
Emory and Henry College, Emory, VA 24327
Ferrum College, Ferrum, VA 24088
George Mason University, Fairfax, VA 22030
Hampden-Sydney College, Hampden-Sydney,
  VA 23943
Hampton University, Hampton, VA 23668
Hollins College, Roanoke, VA 24020
James Madison University, Harrisonburg, VA 22807
Liberty University, Lynchburg, VA 24506
Lynchburg College, Lynchburg, VA 24501
Mary Baldwin College, Staunton, VA 24401
Marymount University, Arlington, VA 22207
Mary Washington College, Fredericksburg, VA 22401
Norfolk State University, Norfolk, VA 23504
Radford University, Radford, VA 24142
Randolph-Macon College, Ashland, VA 23005
Roanoke College, Salem, VA 24153
Sweet Briar College, Sweet Briar, VA 24595
University of Richmond, Richmond, VA 23173
University of Virginia, Charlottesville, VA 22906
Virginia Commonwealth University, Richmond,
  VA 23284
Virginia Military Institute, Lexington, VA 24450
Virginia Polytechnic Institute and State University,
  Blacksburg, VA 24061
Virginia Wesleyan College, Norfolk, VA 23502
Washington and Lee University, Lexington, VA 24450

Data Processing
Blue Ridge Community College, Weyers Cave,
  VA 24486

171

Central Virginia Community College, Lynchburg,
  VA 24502
Dabney S. Lancaster Community College, Clifton
  Forge, VA 24422
Eastern Shore Community College, Melfa, VA 23410
Germanna Community College, Locust Grove,
  VA 22508
J. Sargeant Reynolds Community College, Richmond,
  VA 23261
New River Community College, Dublin, VA 24084
Patrick Henry Community College, Martinsville,
  VA 24115
Paul D. Camp Community College, Franklin, VA 23851
Piedmont Virginia Community College, Charlottesville,
  VA 22901
Southside Virginia Community College, Alberta,
  VA 23821
Thomas Nelson Community College, Hampton,
  VA 23670
Tidewater Community College, Portsmouth, VA 23703
Virginia Highlands Community College, Abingdon,
  VA 24210
Virginia Western Community College, Roanoke,
  VA 24038
Wytheville Community College, Wytheville, VA 24382

WASHINGTON

Computer Science
Central Washington University, Ellensburg, WA 98926
Eastern Washington University, Cheney, WA 99004
Evergreen State College, Olympia, WA 98505
Gonzaga University, Spokane, WA 99258
Heritage College, Toppenish, WA 98948
Pacific Lutheran University, Tacoma, WA 98447
St. Martin's College, Lacey, WA 98503

Seattle Pacific University, Seattle, WA 98119
Seattle University, Seattle, WA 98122
University of Puget Sound, Tacoma, WA 98416
University of Washington, Seattle, WA 98195
Walla Walla College, College Place, WA 99324
Washington State University, Pullman, WA 99164
Western Washington University, Bellingham,
    WA 98225
Whitman College, Walla Walla, WA 99362
Whitworth College, Spokane, WA 99251

Data Processing
Bellevue Community College, Bellevue, WA 98007
Big Bend Community College, Moses Lake, WA 98837
Centralia College, Centralia, WA 98531
Clark College, Vancouver, WA 98663
Everett Community College, Everett, WA 98201
Grays Harbor College, Aberdeen, WA 98520
Highline Community College, Des Moines, WA 98198
Lower Columbia College, Longview, WA 98632
North Seattle Community College, Seattle, WA 98103
Olympic College, Bremerton, WA 98310
Peninsula College, Port Angeles, WA 98362
Pierce College, Tacoma, WA 98498
Seattle Central Community College, Seattle, WA 98122
South Puget Sound Community College, Olympia,
    WA 98502
Spokane Community College, Spokane, WA 99207
Tacoma Community College, Tacoma, WA 98465

WEST VIRGINIA

Computer Science
Alderson-Broaddus College, Philippi, WV 26416
Bethany College, Bethany, WV 26032
Bluefield State College, Bluefield, WV 24701

Concord College, Athens, WV 24712
Davis and Elkins College, Elkins, WV 26241
Glenville State College, Glenville, WV 26351
Marshall University, Huntington, WV 25755
Parkersburg Community College, Parkersburg,
    WV 26101
Potomac State College, Keyser, WV 26726
Shepherd College, Shepherdstown, WV 25443
West Virginia Institute of Technology, Montgomery,
    WV 26506
West Virginia State College, Institute, WV 25112
West Virginia University, Morgantown, WV 26506
West Virginia Wesleyan College, Buckhannon,
    WV 26201
Wheeling Jesuit College, Wheeling, WV 26003

Data Processing
Parkersburg Community College, Parkersburg,
    WV 26101
Potomac State College, Keyser, WV 26726
Southern West Virginia College, Logan, WV 25601

WISCONSIN

Computer Science
Alverno College, Milwaukee, WI 53215
Beloit College, Beloit, WI 53511
Cardinal Stritch College, Milwaukee, WI 53217-3985
Carroll College, Waukesha, WI 53186
Lakeland College, Sheboygan, WI 53082
Lawrence University, Appleton, WI 54912
Marquette University, Milwaukee, WI 53233
Mount Mary College, Milwaukee, WI 53222
Northland College, Ashland, WI 54806
Ripon College, Ripon, WI 54971
St. Norbert College, De Pere, WI 54115

174

Silver Lake College, Manitowoc, WI 54220
University of Wisconsin, Madison, WI 53706
Viterbo College, La Crosse, WI 54601

Data Processing
Blackhawk Technical College, Janesville, WI 53547
Gateway Technical College, Kenosha, WI 53144
Lakeshore Technical College, Cleveland, WI 53015
Madison Area Technical College, Madison, WI 53704
Mid-State Technical College, Wisconsin Rapids,
    WI 54494
Milwaukee Area Technical College, Milwaukee,
    WI 53233
Nicolet Area Technical College, Rhinelander, WI 54501
Northcentral Technical College, Wausau, WI 54401
Northeast Wisconsin Technical College, Green Bay,
    WI 54307
Waukesha County Technical College, Pewaukee,
    WI 53072
Western Wisconsin Technical College, La Crosse,
    WI 54602

WYOMING

Computer Science
Casper College, Casper, WY 82601
Laramie County Community College, Cheyenne,
    WY 82007
Northwest Community College, Powell, WY 85435
Western Wyoming Community College, Rock Springs,
    WY 82902

Data Processing
Northwest Community College, Powell, WY 85435
Western Wyoming Community College, Rock Springs,
    WY 82901

175

Appendix C
Glossary of Computer Terms

access code   Unique combination of letters or numbers used to gain access to a computer network or online service. Sometimes called *user name* or *user ID and password*.

active file   File in use that any currently issued command will affect.

add-on   Device, such as an external hard disk, that will expand the capacity and capabilities of a computer system.

algorithm   Set of rules or instructions for carrying out a particular task. A recipe in a cookbook, for example, could be considered an algorithm.

algorithmic language   Any programming language that focuses on problem-solving by using algorithms. BASIC, C, FORTRAN and Pascal are examples of algorithmic languages.

alphanumeric   Describing a data field that can hold both letters and numerals.

analog computers   Computers typically used for scientific and industrial operations that do not store data as digital bits but instead represent variable quantities (such as temperature) with a proportionally variable current or voltage.

application   Computer program designed to help people perform a certain type of work, such as payroll, order entry, or word processing. An application can manipulate text, numbers, graphics, or a combination of these elements.

application program   Single, user-written program designed to accomplish a specific user task.

architecture   General term for the structure of all or part of a computer system.

arithmetic logic unit (ALU)   Hardware in the computer containing the circuits and memory that perform arithmetic, comparative, and logical functions.

artificial intelligence (AI)   Branch of computer science that deals with programming computers to process information like humans, using deduction, inference, and the ability to learn from past experience.

ASCII (pronounced "askee")   Acronym for American Standard Code for Information Interchange, a standardized code that enables computers and computer programs to exchange information.

Assembly language   Low-level, machine-oriented programming language in which each statement corresponds directly to a single machine instruction. It is difficult and time-consuming to code but produces very fast and efficient programs.

audit trail   The series of printed computer reports that are produced during processing to show that no errors or omissions have occurred from first input to final output.

backup   The process of storing a duplicate copy of files or programs on a disk or magnetic tape to be available if the original is damaged or erased.

BASIC   Acronym for Beginner's All-purpose Symbolic Instruction Code. The most popular high-level, English-like programming language, it is often taught to beginning programmers because it is easy to use and understand.

batch   Group of documents or data records that are processed as a unit.

batch processing   On microcomputers, the running of a batch file, a stored "batch" of operating system

177

commands carried out one after the other without intervention. On larger computers, batch processing involves acquiring programs and data from users, running them one or a few at a time, and then providing the results.

baud Unit of measurement used to indicate the transmission speed of data over telephone lines.

binary number system The standard number system used on all digital computers. It uses only the digits 0 and 1, which can be represented as the OFF and ON states of a bit of electronic memory.

bit (binary digit) The smallest unit of information processed and stored by a computer. It is either a 0 or a 1 in the binary number system.

block Multiple data records handled as a single group for efficient transfer into and out of memory.

branch Programming technique in which control is passed to an instruction that is not the next sequential instruction in the program.

buffer Temporary storage area for data that helps to compensate for the difference in speed between mechanical and electronic devices in the computer's hardware configuration.

bug Error in software or hardware. In software, a bug causes a program to malfunction or to produce incorrect results. In hardware, a bug is a recurring physical problem that prevents a system or set of components from working together properly.

byte Unit of information containing 8 bits. It is the amount of memory used to store a single character, such as a letter, a numeral, or a punctuation mark.

C Structured programming language that is considered the closest thing to a standard programming language in the microcomputer/workstation marketplace.

CAD (computer-aided design) Programs used in

designing engineering, architectural, and scientific models, ranging from tools to buildings to airplanes.

calculator   Device that performs arithmetic operations on numbers but requires continual interactive instructions from the operator.

cardreader   An input device. Magnetic card readers read information that has been magnetically encoded on a plastic card, like a credit card. Punched-card readers read computer data from punched cards.

cathode-ray tube (CRT)   Large, electronic vacuum tube, similar to a television tube, that is used to display information or data quickly on a microcomputer screen.

CD-ROM (compact disk read-only memory)   Form of high-capacity data storage that uses laser optics for reading data.

central processing unit (CPU)   The electronic "brain" of the computer, which interprets and executes instructions.

clone   Copy. Clones are look-alike, act-alike computers that contain the same microprocessors and run the same programs as better-known, more prestigious, and more expensive machines.

COBOL   Acronym for Common Business Oriented Language. COBOL is a high-level, English-like computer language that is widely accepted and used, especially in business applications.

code   Term for computer instructions.

communication   The transmission of data or information between remote locations.

compile   To translate all the source code of a program from a high-level English-like language into a lower-level, machine-readable format. A program that performs this task is known as a compiler.

computer   Any machine that accepts structured input

179

data, performs calculations and logical operations on that data, and reports the results.

computer-output microfilm (COM) Microfilm that can record data from a computer without the use of a camera for efficient storage of high-volume reports.

computer program Set of instructions in a computer language to be executed on a computer to perform a specific task.

computer science The study of computers, including design, operation, and use.

console The terminal used by the computer user for interactive communication with the computer.

control section The part of the central processing unit that decodes each programmed instruction in proper sequence.

control total The printed sum of a particular field in a group of records, accumulated to ensure the accuracy of the computer processing; part of the audit trail.

control unit Device or circuit that regulates between the computer and one of the peripheral input/output devices.

core-image library A portion of the master system disk library that contains programs in machine language–executable form.

crash The sudden failure of either a program or a disk drive.

data Any collection of characters—numeric or alphabetic—that can be assigned a meaning and processed by a computer to produce meaningful information.

database File comprising related, integrated records together with a collection of operations that facilitate searching, sorting, recombination, and other activities.

database management system (DBMS) Set of software programs for creating, modifying, updating, and retrieving information in a database system.

data entry The process of writing new data into computer memory, typically from a keyboard.

data file File consisting of data—text, numbers, or graphics—as distinct from a program file of executable instructions.

data processing (DP) Work performed by computers: the inputting of data, the application of a series of changes leading to a result, and the reporting of that result in the form of useful information.

data transfer The movement of information from one location to another, either within a computer or between a computer and an external device (as between two computers).

debug To use software to detect, locate, and correct errors in a computer program.

decimal numbering system Numbering system using the base 10 and the digits 0 through 9.

desk checking Tracing the various paths though a program to verify the logic before submitting it for a computer test.

desktop publishing Use of a computer and specialized software to combine text and graphics to create a document that can be printed on a laser printer or a typesetting machine.

digital computer The dominant variety of computer for both scientific and business applications. Data are stored in a digital computer in binary form, as a series of 1s and 0s.

direct access The ability of a computer to go straight to a particular storage location in memory or on a disk and retrieve or store an item of information. Also called *random access*.

disk memory Semipermanent data storage on a disk.

181

disk pack   High-volume storage device consisting of a collection of disks in plastic housing. Data are stored magnetically on the surface of the disk, which is used for both input and output.

display   The visual output device of a computer.

distributed processing   Form of information processing where work is performed by individual computers that are linked through a communications network.

documentation   The flowcharts, logic narratives, truth tables, and other written instructions that explain the functioning of a computer system or program.

dump   Automatic printout of main memory that occurs when a program fails during processing. The dump will assist the programmer who must debug the program logic.

electronic data processing (EDP)   See *data processing.*

electronic funds transfer (EFT)   The transfer of "magnetic money" over phone lines from one bank to another.

electronic mail   Transmission of messages over a communications network; also called *e-mail.*

encode   To change alphabetic and numeric characters into computer code by setting various patterns of bits to 0 or 1. Some common codes are octal, hexadecimal, and binary.

field   Location in a record in which one data item, made up of one or more characters, is stored.

file   Collection of related records. For example, if a name, address, and phone number make up a record, the phone book would be a file.

file maintenance   The process of using a program to alter a file by inserting, deleting, changing, or copying.

first-generation computers   The first electronic computers, characterized by the use of vacuum tubes.

flowchart   Chart that shows the movement of data

through a program or within a computer system. A flowchart uses agreed-upon symbols such as squares, diamonds, and ovals to describe pictorially various operations.

FORTRAN Acronym for FORmula TRANslation, the first high-level, English-like programming language. It is used heavily in scientific and engineering fields.

freeware Computer program given away free of charge, often through computer bulletin boards or user groups.

general-purpose language Programming language, like BASIC or C, designed for a variety of applications.

hacker Person engrossed in computer programming and computer technology.

hardware The physical computer and related equipment, including printers, modems, and mice.

hexadecimal Numbering system with the base of 16 that consists of digits 0 through 9 and the upper- or lower-case letters A through F.

high-level programming language English-like language that facilitates programming; however, the program must then be translated by a compiler program into machine language the computer understands. Examples are COBOL, FORTRAN, and BASIC.

home computer Personal computer designed for home use and usually available at a lower price than an office PC.

housekeeping The functions performed in the first paragraph of a high-level program, such as setting counters to zero, opening files, and checking labels.

hypertext Medium in which images, sounds, and actions are linked together in such a way that a user can browse through related topics in any order.

information Processed data present in a usable form.

input Data entered into a computer for processing.

input/output (I/O) The tasks of gathering data for the computer to process (usually entering it using a keyboard or mouse) and making the results available to the viewer (usually with a display or printer).

instruction set Group of machine instructions in a given computer language that a microprocessor recognizes and can execute.

integrated circuit (IC) Highly miniaturized electronic chip that contains thousands of transistors and other electronic components.

intelligent terminal Terminal with its own memory and microprocessor.

interactive program Program that interacts with the user, who uses a keyboard, mouse, or joystick to provide responses to the program. A computer game, for example, is an interactive program.

job control language (JCL) Special programming language that controls the computer's operating system as it executes application programs.

job step Single-application program, usually one of many executed sequentially in the jobstream.

joystick Pointing device used to play computer games and for other tasks.

K abbreviation for *kilo-*. In computing, K stands for 1024 characters of main storage (often rounded to 1000). For example, 64K would be read as 64,000 bytes of memory.

key The field in a record used to identify the record, to retrieve it directly from a disk, and sometimes to sort it. In payroll application, employees' social security numbers often are used as keys.

keyboard Part of a computer that resembles a type-writer and is used to input data.

keypunch Device used to punch data holes into paper cards to provide data for early computers.

label Word, symbol, or group of characters used to

identify a file, a storage medium, or an element defined in a computer program.

language processor Computer program that accepts instructions written in a particular computer language and translates them into machine language. Also called a compiler, interpreter, or assembler.

leased line A dedicated or leased telephone channel for private use. A leased line is faster, quieter, and generally more expensive than a standard switched line. Leased lines usually are used for data communications.

light pen Light-sensitive pointing device that can be attached to a computer. The user can hold the wand up to the screen to select items or choose commands instead of typing these selections on a keyboard.

linkage editor (or **linker**) Manufacturer-supplied program that links datafiles and compiled modules to create an executable program.

low-level language Language that corresponds closely to the computer's instruction set, such as machine language or Assembly language.

machine code (or **machine language**) The only language computers understand. High-level languages like BASIC or Pascal are ways of structuring the human language so people can program computers to perform specific tasks. A compiler translates these high-level languages into machine code.

magnetic core (or **core**) An early type of computer memory. A core consisted of small iron circles strung on control wires and magnetized to represent either binary 0 or 1. Now the term is sometimes used to refer to main memory of any computer system.

magnetic disk (or **computer disk**) Flat, circular, metallic plate coated with a material that can be magnetized. The two main types are hard disks and floppy disks or floppies.

magnetic-ink character recognition (MICR) A reliable method of character recognition that reads characters printed with magnetically charged ink. An example of magnetically charged characters are the numbers at the bottom of bank checks.

magnetic tape (or **tape**) A reel of tape with an oxide surface that can be magnetized to store data. On personal computer systems, ordinary two-reel audio cassettes often are used for this purpose.

mainframe computer High-level computer designed for complex and intensive computational tasks. The most powerful mainframes are called supercomputers and are used heavily by researchers in science, big business, and the military.

main storage (or **primary storage**) The central general-purpose storage region of a modern digital computer. Secondary storage options include both disks and tapes.

management information system (MIS) Group of business software systems designed to assist management in decision-making and long-range planning.

mass storage Generic term for disk, tape, or optical disk storage of computer data. Large amounts of data can be stored on these secondary storage devices in comparison with computer memory capacity.

master file Large file stored on disk or tape, which is updated periodically (usually weekly or monthly) and reflects the ongoing financial history of a company.

megabyte (MB) About one million bytes of memory or storage (exactly 1,048,576 bytes).

microcomputer Computer built around a single-chip microprocessor. Less powerful than minicomputers or mainframe computers.

minicomputer Mid-level computer built to perform complex computations, usually used in business or scientific fields.

modem (MOdulator/DEModulator) Device used to transmit electronic data over telephone lines.

modular programming Technique that involves dividing a large computer program into simple functional units. This speeds up the programming process by allowing several programmers to work on a single program at the same time.

monitor The screen on which images generated by the computer's video adapter are displayed.

mouse Common pointing device used to select items or choose commands on the computer screen. The user presses one of the mouse's buttons, producing a "mouse click" to make a selection.

multiplexing Electronic process that allows two or more data transmissions to share a telephone line.

multiprocessing The linking of two computer systems to allow the processing of two programs simultaneously. Each processing unit works on a different set of instructions.

multiprogramming Executing two programs at the same time on one central processing unit by rapidly switching back and forth between them.

nanosecond (NS) One billionth of a second, time measure used to represent computing speed.

natural language Human languages, as opposed to programming or machine languages.

network Group of computers and other devices that are connected by cables, telephones, or other communication links.

numbering system System for the writing and manipulation of numbers using agreed-upon symbols and rules. Examples include decimal, binary, octal, and hexadecimal numbering systems.

object code The complete machine-language program that can be directly executed by a computer's central processing unit.

octal numbering system Numbering system using a base of 8 and the digits 0 through 7.

offline State in which a device, like a printer, cannot communicate with or be controlled by a computer.

online State in which a device is activated and ready for operation, capable of communicating with or being controlled by a computer.

online direct access system Data processing operation controlled by the main computer with files stored on disk, using the direct-access method for high-speed retrieval.

operating system (OS) The manufacturer-supplied master program responsible for controlling the allocation and usage of hardware resources, such as memory, central processing unit time, disk space, and peripheral devices. Popular operating systems include MS-DOS, the Macintosh OS, OS/2, and UNIX.

operation code (or **opcode**) The part of an Assembly language or machine language instruction that tells what operation is to be performed.

optical character recognition (OCR) Process of examining printed characters—such as newspaper articles—and determining their shapes by detecting light and dark. Once the shapes are determined, they are translated into computer text.

original equipment manufacturer (OEM) Firm that incorporates the products of another company into its retail product. Also, a software house that adds specialized software to a minicomputer and retails a complete turnkey system.

output The results of computer processing.

page A fixed-size block of memory.

paging A technique of implementing virtual storage. The virtual address space is divided into fixed-size blocks of memory (pages). These pages can be mapped onto any of the physical addresses available on the system.

parallel interface Hard-wired interface between two devices that transmits all bits in a byte at the same time.

parity Error-checking procedure that verifies the accuracy of data by adding the number of bits that are set ON (the binary 1s) in each byte.

Pascal Concise, structured programming language that gained popularity during the 1980s as a standard development language on microcomputers.

peripheral Term for devices like disk drives, printers, modems, and joysticks that are connected to and controlled by a computer.

personal computer (PC) Computer designed for use by one person at a time.

PL/I Acronym for Programming Language I, a language developed by IBM to combine the best features of COBOL, ALGOL, and FORTRAN, while introducing new concepts. The result was a structured language so complex that it met with only limited acceptance. It is still used, however, in some academic and research environments.

plotter Output device that can produce graphic drawings, including charts and diagrams, using either pens or electrostatic charges and toner. Pen plotters draw on paper with one or more colored pens. Electrostatic plotters "draw" a pattern of electrostatically charged dots on paper and then apply toner to fuse it into place.

plug-compatible manufacturer Company that produces peripherals that can easily be plugged into a popular main computer.

point of sale (POS) The technique of using computerized transaction systems (or online cash registers) to capture sale and inventory data at the moment of sale.

portable computer Any computer designed to be moved easily, ranging from less than 2 pounds to about 30 pounds. Types include transportable, laptop, ultralight, and hand-held.

printer Output device that puts text or a computer-generated image on paper or on another medium, such as a transparency.

private line See *leased line*.

program Series of instructions that can be executed by a computer.

program maintenance Modifying an operational program for the purpose of correcting errors in logic or updating constants in the program to meet changing government regulations or business practices. An example would be changing the amount of federal taxes deducted from employees' paychecks in a payroll program.

programmer Person who writes and debugs computer programs.

random access memory (RAM) Semiconductor-based memory that can be read or written by the micro-processor or other hardware devices.

read-only memory (ROM) Semiconductor-based memory that contains instructions or data that can be read but not modified.

real storage The amount of random access memory (RAM) storage in a computer, as opposed to virtual storage; also called *physical storage* or *physical memory*.

real-time processing The processing of data so quickly through online techniques that the computer output accurately reflects the current state of the data in the real world. An example is stock prices, which change continually throughout the trading day; some computers are designed and programmed to give users up-to-the-second stock prices.

record   Collection of related fields or data items.

register   A small, high-speed part of memory in the computer used to hold specific pieces of data related to activities going on within the system.

remote terminal   Terminal that is at a distant location from the main computer to which it is attached. Remote terminals are connected to main computers by telephone lines.

report generator   Program that uses a report "form" created by the user to lay out and print the contents of a database.

response time   The time between input and output in an online system.

robot   Machine that can sense and react to input and cause changes in its surroundings with some degree of intelligence. Robots rarely are human-like in appearance but often mimic human movements in carrying out their work.

second-generation computer   Computer that uses discrete transistors as its basic circuitry element.

secondary storage   Any data storage other than a computer's random access memory, usually a tape or disk.

segmentation   The technique of dividing a large program into pieces in order to run it on a small computer.

semiconductor   A substance—usually silicon or germanium—that ranks between a conductor and a nonconductor in its ability to conduct electricity.

sequential processing   Processing in the order in which the items of information are stored or input.

service programs   Manufacturer-supplied utility programs that assist in the preparation or execution of

191

user-written programs. Examples are the compiler, the assembler, the linkage editor, and the sort/merge.

software   Computer programs.

solid logic technology   A technique of hardware construction introduced by IBM in the third generation of computers, characterized by the use of integrated circuits to achieve extremely high circuit density.

sort/merge program   Manufacturer-supplied program to sort or merge files by whatever key field and sequence the user specifies.

source code   Human-readable program statements.

source program   The human-readable program written by the programmer that will be input to the compiler.

speech recogition   The ability of a computer to understand the spoken word for the purpose of receiving commands and data input from the speaker.

spooling   A technique of storing data in a disk or memory buffer until the printer is ready to process it.

storage   Device on which computer data can be kept.

structured programming   Technique that produces programs with clear design according to a top-down, modular scheme. Structured programming makes program maintenance easier and makes the program less difficult to read.

supercomputer   Large, extremely fast, and very expensive computer used for complex calculations.

superconductor   Substance that has no resistance to flows of electricity.

supervisor   Another name for *operating system.*

system flowchart   Large pictorial diagram that shows the relationship between programs in a computer system.

systems analyst   Person who works with users to design and develop computer systems.

telecommunications   The transmission of information

—data, television pictures, sound, facsimiles, etc.— over telephone lines or cables.

teleprocessing The use of computers and communications equipment to access computers and computer files located elsewhere.

testing The preliminary running of a program with test data to ensure that it is functioning properly before putting that program into live production.

third-generation computer Computer based on integrated circuits rather than on separately wired transistors.

thrashing The wasteful swapping of pages in and out of virtual storage rather than executing applications.

throughput The data processing rate in a computer system.

time-sharing The use of a computer system by many persons at the same time. Users work at various terminals, and the computer system runs their separate programs concurrently.

top-down design Planning of a system or program in a functional manner so that the most important functions are handled first and the highest level of detail is handled last.

turnaround time The elapsed time between the submission of computer input and the production of output.

turnkey system A finished system with all the hardware, software, and documentation installed and ready for use.

utility program Program designed to perform maintenance work on the system or on system components, for example, a file recovery program.

virtual machine The use of systems software to make one computer system perform like a different computer system.

virtual storage   Technique of using disk space to supplement semiconductor memory.

voice input   Vocal instructions translated by a computer into commands it can execute.

word length   The number of characters in a single computer word, typically 8, 16, or 32. Word length determines the limit of addressable memory.

word processing (WP)   Use of an application program for preparation of textual materials like letters, reports, newspapers, magazines, and books.

Index

knowledge engineering, AI, 3,
112–113
knowledge processing, 111
Kurzweil Applied Intelligence, 4

L
language
AI, 3, 108
computer, 15, 44–48
interactive, 46, 104
machine, 44–45, 62
user, 46
linguistics, 111
laptop, 54
LISP, 3, 108
Lotus, 1-2-3, 5, 93
Spreadsheet, 109

M
mainframe, 55, 56
management, 12, 70–71
information system, 3
line, 38–39
science, 30
strategic, 39
tactical, 39
manager, 3, 31, 37
systems, 77–81
memory, 31, 47, 54, 62, 104
microcode, 42
microcomputer, 50, 53–54, 55
desktop, 55
microprocessor, 42, 53
minicomputer, 11, 50, 55–56
model-building, 30
modem, 6
mystique, programming, 50
myths, programming, 48–50

N
Natural Language Software,
107–111
NCR, 11
NET-TALK, 103–104
neural network, 103–107

NeuroComputers, 107–108
neuron, artificial, 104, 107, 113
Newton, 100

O
object code, 63
operations research, 30
operator, computer, 13–14, 17–18,
22, 57, 65
intervention by, 31
optical character recognition
(OCR), 4

P
palmtop, 55
Pascal, 64
pattern recognition, 3, 4
peripherals, 55
personal computer (PC), 2–6, 14,
100, 107–113
Personal Digital Assistant (PDA),
100
Personal Robot (PR), 106
personnel, 10–11
evaluation, 22, 34–35, 37
turnover, 40
Pert Chart, 38
PL/1, 14, 64
Point of Sale (POS) System, 79–80
Postscript, 5
primary storage unit, 58
printer, 5, 57
problem-solving
business, 15, 63
computer program, 23, 42, 69
program
complexity, 41
design, 22, 31
developing a, 60–65
failure, 32–33, 41, 42
utility, 60
programmer, 3, 12–15, 19–21,
30–52, 64
junior, 84–89
trainee, 37, 77